EUCHARISTIC ADORATION

PRAYER BOOK

EUCHARISTIC ADORATION
PRAYER BOOK

Written and compiled by Marie Paul Curley, FSP

Edited by Mary Leonora Wilson, FSP

auline
BOOKS & MEDIA
Boston

Nihil Obstat: Reverend Joseph Briody, S.S.L., S.T.D.

Imprimatur: ✠ Seán P. Cardinal O'Malley, O.F.M. Cap.
Archbishop of Boston
May 10, 2023

Library of Congress Cataloging-in-Publication Data Number: 2023935998

ISBN 0-8198-2414-3

ISBN 978-0-8198-2414-1

Scripture quotations contained herein, excluding psalms and canticles and where otherwise indicated, are from the *New Revised Standard Version Bible: Catholic Edition*, copyright © 1989, 1993, Division of Christian Education of the National Council of the Churches of Christ in the United States of America. Used by permission. All rights reserved.

All psalms and canticles are from The *ESV*® Bible (*The Holy Bible, English Standard Version*®), copyright © 2001 by Crossway, a publishing ministry of Good News Publishers. Used by permission. All rights reserved. The ESV text may not be quoted in any publication made available to the public by a Creative Commons license. The *ESV* may not be translated in whole or in part into any other language.

Scriptures where indicated are taken from the *New American Bible*, revised edition © 2010, 1991, 1986, 1970 Confraternity of Christian Doctrine, Washington, DC, and are used by permission of the copyright owner. All rights reserved. No part of the New American Bible may be reproduced in any form without permission in writing from the copyright owner.

Excerpts from papal and magisterial texts copyright © Dicastero per la Comunicazione-Libreria Editrice Vaticana.

Cover design and art by Kenneth Reaume

All rights reserved. No part of this book may be reproduced or transmitted in any form or by any means, electronic or mechanical, including photocopying, recording, or by any information storage and retrieval system, without permission in writing from the publisher.

"P" and PAULINE are registered trademarks of the Daughters of St. Paul.

Copyright © 2024, Daughters of St. Paul

Published by Pauline Books & Media, 50 Saint Pauls Avenue, Boston, MA 02130–3491

Printed in South Korea.

www.pauline.org

Pauline Books & Media is the publishing house of the Daughters of St. Paul, an international congregation of women religious serving the Church with the communications media.

1 2 3 4 5 6 7 8 9   29 28 27 26 25 24

Contents

Preface: The Invitation, "Come to Me" . . . . *xix*

Introduction: The Gift of the Eucharist and
   How to Use This Book *1*

Part One

Introduction to Eucharistic Adoration

The Importance of Eucharistic Prayer *9*

Adoring Jesus in the Sacrament of Love *11*

Pauline Spirituality *14*

Part Two

Source and Summit of Our Christian Life

The Mass *25*

  Preparing for Mass and Communion *27*

  Prayers Before Mass *31*

    Offering of the Holy Mass *31*

    A Eucharistic Offertory for the Media *32*

Prayers Before Communion 35
    Act of Faith, Hope, and Love 35
    Prayer of Saint Ambrose Before Communion 36
    Prayer of Love and Humility 38
    Prayer of Gratitude and Faith 39
    Act of Desire 39
    Come, Lord Jesus 40
    Prayer for Love 40
    Act of Love and Desire 41
    Eucharistic Offering 43
    Act of Spiritual Communion 43

Prayers After Communion 44
    Act of Adoration 44
    Act of Resolution 45
    Act of Supplication 45
    Thanksgiving for the Gift of the Eucharist 46
    Act of Thanksgiving 47
    I Will Remain with You 47
    Prayer for Perseverance 48
    I Am Not Worthy 49
    Soul of Christ 50
    Anima Christi 51
    Acts of Adoration, Thanksgiving, Reparation, and Prayer . . . 52
    Litany of Holy Communion 53

Benediction 59
    O Saving Victim 60
    O Salutaris Hostia 61
    Humbly Let Us Voice Our Homage 62
    Tantum Ergo 63
    The Divine Praises 64

How to Live a Eucharistic Day 65

Part Three
Holy Hour Guides

The Pauline Hour of Adoration 71
    How to Make a Pauline Hour of Adoration 71

Holy Hour One
Encountering the Master 77

Holy Hour Two
Bread of Life 85

Holy Hour Three
Jesus Our Way, Truth, and Life 93

Holy Hour Four
Jesus, Word of Life 101

HOLY HOUR FIVE
With Jesus Crucified *109*

HOLY HOUR SIX
"I Am with You" *115*

HOLY HOUR SEVEN
Praising God with Christ, Our Risen Savior *123*

HOLY HOUR EIGHT
Called by Jesus the Good Shepherd *131*

HOLY HOUR NINE
Eucharistic Disciples *139*

HOLY HOUR TEN
Mary, Woman of the Eucharist *147*

PART FOUR

Treasury of Prayers

Biblical Prayers *157*

    Psalm 23 . . . . *161*

    Psalm 31 . . . . *162*

    Psalm 51 . . . . *164*

    Psalm 63 . . . . *166*

    Psalm 100 . . . . *167*

  Psalm 116 . . . . *167*

  Psalm 118 . . . . *169*

  Psalm 130 . . . . *172*

  Psalm 139 . . . . *172*

  Canticle of Isaiah 55 . . . . *175*

  Benedictus *177*

  Magnificat *178*

  Jesus' Priestly Prayer *179*

  Canticle of Ephesians 1 . . . . *181*

  Canticle of 1 Peter *182*

  Canticle of Revelation 19 . . . . *183*

Prayers of Adoration *185*

  Morning Offering *185*

  Prayer of Adoration *186*

  Prayer of Presence *187*

  You *187*

  Chaplet to Jesus Master, Way, Truth, and Life *188*

  Chaplet of Eucharistic Adoration *191*

  Bread of My Soul *192*

  Immersed in Adoration *193*

  We Adore You *193*

  Beloved Jesus *194*

  Stay with Me, Lord *194*

  Act of Abandonment *195*

Act of Adoration	*196*
Litany of the Most Blessed Sacrament	*197*
Credo, Adoro, Amo	*200*
Loving Lord, I Believe	*201*
Prayer Before the Blessed Sacrament	*202*

Prayers of Praise and Thanksgiving *205*

O Sacrament Most Holy	*206*
May the Heart of Jesus	*206*
Thanks Be to Thee	*206*
You Have First Loved Me	*207*
Filled with Wonder	*207*
Forever Yours	*208*
Te Deum	*209*
Novena of Grace	*211*
A Grateful Heart	*211*
O Immense Love!	*212*
Prayer of Thanksgiving	*212*
Praise of God's Love	*213*
Litany of the Eucharist	*213*

Prayers of Repentance and Reparation *217*

Act of Contrition	*217*
The Jesus Prayer	*218*
Be Merciful	*218*
Possess Our Hearts	*218*

Too Late Have I Loved You 219

Litany of Repentance 220

Repentance and Reunion 220

To Jesus Good Shepherd 221

Litany of the Precious Blood 222

Angel of Fatima's Prayers of Reparation 224

Litany of Reparation to the Most Holy Sacrament 225

Act of Reparation to the Most Blessed Sacrament 228

Stations of the Cross 229

To Jesus Crucified 235

The Sacrament of Reconciliation 236

Prayers of Intercession and Petition 239

As I Walk in Your Light 240

God's Dream for Me 240

For Faith in the Real Presence 241

Prayer for the Gifts of the Holy Spirit 242

To My Guardian Angel, Companion in Adoration 243

Act of Trust in the Divine Master 244

Heart of Love 245

Prayer of Saint Francis 245

Prayer of Surrender 246

Shine Through Me 246

Soul of Jesus 247

Come, Holy Spirit 248

For Protection and Enlightenment *249*
Prayer for the Needs of Others *249*
In Our Daily Living *250*
Prayer for Priests *250*
To Foster Respect for Life *251*
Prayer of Saint Gertrude for the Souls in Purgatory *252*
Divine Mercy Chaplet *252*
Invocations to the Eucharistic Heart of Jesus *253*

In Adoration with Mary *257*
The Mysteries of the Rosary: Eucharistic Reflections *258*
Eucharistic Mysteries of the Rosary *270*
Litany of Loreto *274*
Our Lady of the Most Blessed Sacrament *277*
The Angelus *277*
Memorare *278*
We Fly to Your Protection *279*
Hail, Holy Queen *279*
O Mary, My Queen *279*
Act of Consecration *280*
Prayer to the Mother of All Adorers *281*
Hail Mary, of Whom Was Born Our Eucharistic Jesus *281*
Prayer to Increase Eucharistic Devotion *282*
Invocation for the Eucharistic Kingdom of Christ *282*
O Mary, Make Me an Apostle *283*

  Prayer of Entrustment 283
  Prayer to Mary for Families 284

Favorite Eucharistic Hymns 285
  Soul of My Savior 285
  O Sacrum Convivium! 286
  Ave Verum 286
  O Sacred Banquet 287
  Hail, True Body 287
  Godhead Here in Hiding 288
  Panis Angelicus 290
  Bread of Angels 291
  Sing My Tongue the Savior's Glory 292
  Pange Lingua 293
  O Esca Viatorum 296
  O Food of All Wayfaring 297
  Let All Mortal Flesh Keep Silence 298
  Jesus, Food of Angels 299
  O God of Loveliness 299
  Be Thou My Vision 301

Acknowledgments 303

Notes 307

List of Contributors 313

Preface

The Invitation, "Come to Me"

God longs to be close to you. Perhaps that seems too incredible, but with the light of faith we know it is true, as the word of God tells us, many times and in many ways.

Jesus invites us into this closeness with himself:

> "Come to me, all you that are weary and are carrying heavy burdens, and I will give you rest. Take my yoke upon you, and learn from me; for I am gentle and humble in heart, and you will find rest for your souls. For my yoke is easy, and my burden is light." (Mt 11:28–30)

Jesus' gift of his very self in the Eucharist is an ongoing, amazing manifestation of God's eagerness to be not just close, but united with *you*.

In their prayer, mystics have heard Jesus express this desire, even beg for our love, with astonishing vehemence. Saints such as John the Evangelist, Paul the Apostle, Gertrude the Great, Margaret Mary Alacoque, and so many more have shared their insight into God's tremendous yearning for personal intimacy with us. How else can the gift of the Holy Eucharist to the Church be explained?

Even though I was raised in a Catholic family where Mass and Communion were an essential part of life, I didn't start to fall in love with Jesus in the Holy Eucharist until my first visit to the convent of the Daughters of Saint Paul, where I joined the sisters for an hour of adoration. That deeply familiar time with Jesus drew me with a force that I could not—and still cannot—explain. Over the next few months, the sisters' daily hour of adoration became instrumental in helping me recognize that God was calling me to enter the congregation of the Daughters of Saint Paul.

The Holy Eucharist didn't only draw me to my vocation. Jesus' ever-present faithfulness has been my joy, my refuge, my strength, my inspiration, and my motivation: truly the Light of my life. Even on those days when I feel overwhelmed by horrific events or the sufferings in the world, making a visit to Jesus in the Blessed Sacrament always roots me in what is most important: God's saving love for me and all humanity, a love ever-faithful and at work in my life and the world. Somehow, I can always take the next step forward with him.

Deepening your relationship with Jesus in the Eucharist is a privileged way to grow closer to God. Countless people have found fulfillment, serenity, strength, wisdom, and wholeness in Eucharistic adoration.

The *Eucharistic Adoration Prayer Book* is both an introduction to adoration for those just starting this beautiful practice, and a resource and invaluable guide for those seeking to renew or deepen their adoration in a way that fosters spiritual growth, wholeness, and holiness. Although I have written and edited several books on the Holy Eucharist, this edition is the most complete resource for Eucharistic prayer that my community and I have ever done.

My prayers and the prayers of the Daughters of Saint Paul accompany you each time you pick up this prayer book: that through your encounters with Jesus in the Holy Eucharist, you may come to realize ever more deeply how very much God longs to be close to you—and not just to you, but to every person on the face of the earth.

SISTER MARIE PAUL CURLEY, FSP

Introduction

The Gift of the Eucharist and How to Use This Book

> The many ways in which Christ is present to us fills our minds with awe. They are a mystery the Church reflects on with wonder. But there is one way in which Christ is present in his Church that is greater than all others. It is his presence in the Sacrament of the Eucharist.
>
> —Pope Saint Paul VI[1]

The Eucharist is God's greatest gift to us—it is where Jesus' Heart meets the needs of the world daily. Although God is present in the world and the Church in many ways, in the Eucharist he is present in a very special way—Body, Blood, soul, and divinity in the Person of Jesus Christ. If we want to deepen our relationship with God, if we want to grow into the persons God created us to be, if we want to fulfill our true potential and make a difference in the lives of those around us, we *need* to be rooted in Jesus in the Eucharist.

We root our lives in the Eucharist by giving priority to Mass and participating fully in this great mystery—

attentively listening to the readings, uniting ourselves with Jesus in his offering to the Father, joyfully receiving Jesus' loving embrace in Holy Communion so that we can go forth to bring Jesus' love to others. When we truly understand what happens at every Mass, the Sunday Eucharist becomes the center of our week. Or if we can attend daily Mass, that sacred time becomes the focal point of our day. Eucharistic adoration, prayer before Jesus in the Blessed Sacrament outside of the Mass, becomes a way to enrich our participation in the Eucharistic Celebration. Eucharistic adoration is an opportune time to immerse ourselves more deeply in the paschal mystery—Jesus' passion, death, and Resurrection—so that we begin to take on Jesus' attitudes, way of life, and love for the Father. The Eucharist is the heart of Catholic life.

Eucharistic adoration is powerfully transforming. The deeper our Eucharistic prayer, the more fully we can participate in the Mass and allow Jesus to transform us—both in the liturgy we celebrate together and in our daily living. This prayer book, drawn from Scripture, the saints, the Church's teaching, and current spiritual writers, offers a comprehensive resource for those who would like to enrich their Eucharistic prayer, as well as for those who would like to begin but aren't sure where to start. Each section of the prayer book is designed for a particular way of praying or for a particular moment of Eucharistic prayer.

Part One: Introduction to Eucharistic Adoration presents the importance of Eucharistic prayer in our lives, as it has been practiced through the centuries and recommended by the saints. This prayer book especially highlights the approach of one "specialist" in Eucharistic prayer, Blessed James Alberione, the Founder of the Pauline Family, whose spirituality is centered around the Eucharistic Master, Christ, who is the Way, Truth, and Life.

Part Two: Source and Summit of our Christian Life delves into the importance of the Mass, with recommendations on how to approach the Eucharistic Celebration in a fresh way every time, and a treasury of prayers that may be helpful before and after Communion. The section concludes with encouragement and tips for centering our day around the Eucharist.

Part Three: Holy Hour Guides offers an introduction on making a holy hour before the Blessed Sacrament according to the spirituality of Blessed James Alberione. This is followed by ten prayer guides on various themes that may be useful to you for an hour of adoration at a time of your choosing.

Part Four: Treasury of Prayers is, in many ways, the heart of this prayer book; it is a compilation of prayers oriented to

Eucharistic adoration—whether for five minutes before Mass or when making a holy hour. This part is divided into the following sections:

> *Praying with the Bible* is highly encouraged during times of Eucharistic adoration. This section offers suggestions for different ways of praying with the word of God, as well as a selection of biblical prayers.
>
> *Prayers of Adoration*, *Prayers of Praise and Thanksgiving*, *Prayers of Repentance and Reparation*, and *Prayers of Intercession and Petition* are based on the classic four purposes of prayer.
>
> *In Adoration with Mary* offers a selection of Marian prayers and reflections on the Rosary. From the moment of her *fiat*, Mary became a living tabernacle of Jesus. At Bethlehem she was the first to adore him. She is our model in adoration, always drawing us closer to her Divine Son.
>
> *Favorite Eucharistic Hymns* is a small collection of some of the most popular traditional Eucharistic hymns that can be prayed silently or sung together.

The Eucharist is an unfathomable gift of divine love. The more we spend time with Jesus in the Eucharist, the more our ways of thinking, acting, and loving gradually become

Christlike. Frequent Eucharistic prayer allows us to glimpse Jesus' own relationship with the Father and the Spirit—and we begin to enter the inner life of the Trinity, embraced in their eternal communion of love! As we deepen our understanding that in Christ we are God's Beloved, we begin to more fully live out our call to bring our world into deeper communion with Jesus and, in him, with the Father and the Spirit.

Part One

Introduction to Eucharistic Adoration

In the Eucharist, the Son of God comes to meet us and desires to become one with us; Eucharistic adoration is simply the natural consequence of the Eucharistic Celebration, which is itself the Church's supreme act of adoration.

—Pope Benedict XVI[2]

The Importance of Eucharistic Prayer

> Then he took a loaf of bread, and when he had given thanks, he broke it and gave it to them, saying, "This is my body, which is given for you. Do this in remembrance of me." And he did the same with the cup after supper, saying, "This cup that is poured out for you is the new covenant in my blood."
>
> —Luke 22:19–20

The Eucharist is Jesus' most personal and precious gift, given to us the evening before he sacrificed his life for our salvation. It is the Lord's astonishingly creative way to remain with us and to accompany us throughout life with his presence and his strength. In a mysterious but very real way, Christ is present in the Blessed Sacrament. Spending time with Jesus in the Eucharist is a special way to grow closer to the Lord who loves you so much. If you are:

- looking for a way to deepen your relationship with God,
- yearning for "something more" in your life,
- wrestling with faith,
- needing light and support for a painful or difficult situation,

o or longing for fulfillment, healing, peace, and wholeness,

then praying in the presence of the Eucharistic Jesus can transform your life!

Catholics worship Jesus in the Eucharist in two ways: by actively participating in the Eucharistic Celebration and through Eucharistic adoration.

The Eucharist "is the source and summit"[3] of life, the highest form of prayer, and the greatest worship we can offer to God. At every Mass, Jesus renews his offering of himself to the Father in his passion, death, and Resurrection—a sacrifice he offered once and for all on our behalf, to save us and ultimately bring us into the life of the Trinity.

"For in the blessed Eucharist is contained the whole spiritual good of the Church, namely Christ himself, our Pasch."[4]

The Eucharistic Celebration defines who we are as followers of Christ, uniting us to Christ and each other, becoming one body in Christ. By participating in the Mass, we fulfill Christ's command, "Do this in memory of me," gradually allowing the saving power of Christ's love to touch and transform every aspect of our lives. From the Eucharist we celebrate, we are sent forth to take Christ's saving message to a world thirsting for God's love, justice, peace, and true freedom.

While the Mass is the high point of our lives and worship, the Church has long encouraged Eucharistic adoration as a privileged time to ponder this tremendous mystery of Christ's self-giving love.

Adoring Jesus in the Eucharist draws each of us deeper into the paschal mystery, strengthening our desire to share in the life, death, and Resurrection of the Lord. Our adoration leads us back to the Mass, better prepared to appreciate its meaning, power, and beauty: to receive the word of God, unite ourselves with Christ's offering of himself to the Father, and receive Jesus in Holy Communion.

Adoring Jesus in the Sacrament of Love

> Christ is on earth today, alive on a thousand altars; and he does solve people's problems exactly as he did when he was on earth. . . . That is, he solves the problems of the limited number of people who choose of their own free will to listen to him.
>
> —G. K. Chesterton[5]

Just as there are as numerous ways to pray, so there are many ways to adore Jesus in the Eucharist. One thing is essential: to place oneself before the Blessed Sacrament. Jesus so longs for your love that the best thing you can do is to speak to him from the depths of your heart and to listen to what comes to you from his Heart. Jesus will be delighted every time you open your heart to him.

But it isn't always easy to do this. While we may desire to enter into personal conversation with Jesus in the tabernacle, sometimes we find obstacles in the way: distractions, a sense that God is distant or too silent, overwhelming worries or emotions, spiritual dryness, or a lack of ease or uncertainty of what to say or how to begin.

Over the centuries, many traditions for Eucharistic prayer have arisen that can make it easier to begin Eucharistic adoration. One common way of making a holy hour is to pray a series of vocal prayers. Many groups who make a holy hour together will do this. The holy hour may include a reading and a sermon, the Liturgy of the Hours, the Rosary, the Divine Mercy Chaplet, litanies, and various hymns. Often, a time of public adoration will conclude with Benediction.

Two methods that flow from the Mass and seem to bear great fruit in the lives of the adorers have been promoted by several saints.

Saint Alphonsus de Liguori and Saint Peter Julian Eymard, among others, encouraged participating at Mass by intentionally focusing on the four purposes of prayer in the Mass: adoration, thanksgiving, repentance, and petition. Saint Peter Julian Eymard then recommended dividing the hour of adoration into fifteen-minute segments, with each quarter of an hour focusing on one of those purposes of prayer. (The *Treasury of Prayers* includes a section for each of these purposes of prayer.)

The second method for Eucharistic adoration based on the Mass was developed and encouraged by Blessed James Alberione. Pauline Eucharistic adoration seeks to help the adorer engage in a dynamic and very personal encounter with Jesus in the Holy Eucharist who is our Way, Truth, and Life. Alberione understood the holy hour as just such an encounter with Christ.

Whatever method you choose, it should always support or deepen your adoration, not distract you. In fact, after describing Pauline adoration in detail and recommending its threefold structure, Blessed James Alberione added:

> There are so many ways to make the Visit to the Blessed Sacrament, but the best way is to make it. . . . And what should you tell Jesus? Everything that comes into your mind and heart, just as the shepherds at the manger did or Nathaniel in Jesus' house. We must go to Jesus and pour out our hearts to Him; this is the way to visit him. If you go to visit your mother, do you first study many different methods or the way to visit her? No, no. You go home. You enter without being invited. You throw your arms around your mother's neck and then you begin speaking eagerly. Do the same with Jesus. Tell him everything with simplicity, without studying methods.[6]

Pauline Spirituality

> For to me, living is Christ and dying is gain.
> —Saint Paul (Philippians 1:21)

The resources in this prayer book rely heavily on the thought, spirituality, and prayers of Blessed James Alberione, which have inspired thousands to embrace and live in the Eucharistic Christ. The following explanation of the Pauline Eucharistic spirituality may be helpful to fully benefit from this prayer book.

The central idea of Pauline spirituality is the full development of the human person in Christ as expressed by Saint Paul: "It is no longer I who live, but it is Christ who lives in me" (Gal 2:20). This transformation of the whole person in Jesus Christ is called *Christification* by Blessed James Alberione. He founded five active religious congregations, and personally directed them and guided their apostolic works.[7] In addition, he founded four secular institutes.[8] His hectic schedule would seem to have left little room for adoration, yet he understood the value of Eucharistic adoration as an essential part of this work of transformation in Christ and of apostolic effectiveness. He often called the hour of adoration one of the most fruitful and formative spiritual practices, because it allows for personal assimilation of the riches of the Mass: "From this vital source, the Eucharistic Master, everything receives life."[9] "[The hour of adoration] prepares one for Holy Mass and Holy Communion. Frequent encounters and familiar conversation with Jesus produce friendship, resemblance, and identity of thought, feeling, and willing with Jesus."[10]

Father Alberione called the hour of adoration "the school of Jesus Master," comparing it to the time the first disciples spent coming to know, love, and follow the loving Master who called them. He also often referred to the hour of adoration as "the Visit," signifying its intimate and intensely personal nature. The Visit with Jesus is a special time when we can simply be present before the Lord, listening to him, and telling him everything in our heart.

Father Alberione's way of adoration is easy to use and very relevant for today in its rich use of Scripture, its flexibility, and its holistic approach. It can be easily adapted to personal prayer styles—both more active forms of prayer and silent contemplation. It also challenges the individual to allow God's word to transform his or her attitudes, choices, and life.

"It Is Christ Who Lives in Me!"

Father Alberione placed the Pauline concept of a central, life-changing relationship with Jesus in the context of Christ's profound self-description, "I am the way, and the truth, and the life" (Jn 14:6). The inspired genius of Father Alberione saw these distinct elements as intrinsically related to each other: as we enter more deeply into a personal relationship with Jesus, our lives are transformed.

The title "Master" describes the personal and unique relationship Jesus has with each of his disciples. In Alberione's words:

> Devotion to Jesus Master sums up and completes all devotions. In fact, it presents Jesus Truth in whom we are to believe; Jesus Way who is to be followed; Jesus Life in whom we should live.... Speaking of Jesus Master, we must keep in mind a much broader sense of this title. He not only communicates knowledge, but he also transfuses his life into the disciples, making them similar to himself. He forms the divine life in them and guides them to eternal life.[11]

A true master is not just an expert, but a teacher, guide, mentor, and model who has a genuine relationship with each disciple. The Master lovingly accompanies and guides each one on the path to the deepest fulfillment of our unique potential.

While the connotations of the word "Master" are not always positive, Jesus overturns any negative understanding of mastery and power in a stunning reversal: "You call me 'teacher' and 'master,' and rightly so, for indeed I am. If I, therefore, the master and teacher, have washed your feet, you ought to wash one another's feet" (Jn 13:13–14, NABRE). Indeed, Jesus gave the term "Master" a whole new meaning: Jesus is Master in order to serve (see Lk 22:27). His Lordship over us empowers us to live with the dignity of children of God. Through Jesus, we receive the full freedom and dignity of friendship with God. As our true Master, Jesus is the One who gives the deepest meaning to our lives, and we are his because he loved us into being, died to save us, and constantly reveals his loving care for us.

As the Way, Truth, and Life, Jesus Master profoundly transforms anyone who encounters him. Father Alberione linked Jesus' self-definition to three essential aspects of the person: mind, will, and heart. Jesus sanctifies our minds by revealing the deepest Truth about God and the human person, our wills by being our Way to happiness, and our hearts by offering us the eternal Life for which we yearn.

Jesus, the Truth that Sets Us Free

In the Gospels, it is easy to see how Jesus the Divine Master teaches us important truths so that we can live a happy and holy life. Jesus' words, teaching, Incarnation, life, death, and Resurrection—along with the ongoing teaching of his Spirit-guided Church—are radiant truths that most clearly reveal the mystery of God and our relationship with God. But Jesus' simple statement, "I am the truth" (see Jn 14:6) does not just say he reveals truth; Jesus calls himself *the* Truth. Jesus is the Truth because it is in his very person that we discover the mysterious reality of God: Love emptying itself completely for the sake of the beloved. Jesus does more than tell us what the Father is like; he reveals the very face of God to us by how he relates to us.

When we begin to accept Jesus as the truth of existence and of our very lives, we begin to recognize and take responsibility for our indestructible freedom and dignity as beings made in the image of God. Jesus asks us to respond in faith by acknowledging and committing to the truth. We pray for knowledge, wisdom, insight, and the grace to accept and integrate the truth into our lives. Faith in Jesus can transform our lives.

> We honor Jesus Master, who made himself our wisdom, by placing ourselves humbly at his feet; by listening to what he left us in the Gospel and communicates to us through the Church; by accepting and believing all his teachings; by repeating to him with Saint Peter: "You have the words of eternal life. We have come to believe and know that you are the Holy One of God." (Jn 6:68–69)[12]

Jesus is the ultimate Truth every human person searches for, the saving truth so desperately needed in our world today. Living our call to witness and proclaim Christ demands much of us. We do not need to be afraid, however. Jesus is with us in the struggle. He is not only our Truth, but also our Way.

Jesus, Way to the Father

At the Last Supper Jesus said, "I am the way," inviting his disciples to follow him as the Way to the Father. In other places in the Gospel, Jesus offers himself as our model: "Learn from me" (Mt 11:29) and "Love one another as I have loved you"

(Jn 15:12). Jesus invites us to contemplate him as our Way and to live as he did.

> Jesus willed to be the first one to live the life that we should live; he willed to be the first one to walk the road which would lead us to the Father. . . . He made himself our Way to the Father, becoming our mediator and our brother. . . . This is why it is absolutely necessary to imitate Jesus our model, to make his adoration, his thanksgiving, his reparation, his petitions, our own.[13]

Jesus lived the perfect life, not because it made sense according to society's standards or because everything went his way, but because he fully lived his Father's will. By trusting completely in the Father's loving plan, and by actively cooperating with him in every aspect of his life, Jesus showed us how to live as the Father's beloved sons and daughters.

Jesus shows us the way to the Father both by his words and example, including the Commandments, the Beatitudes, and his new commandment of love. By fully taking on our human nature in his Incarnation, Jesus united himself with every person and sanctified every genuinely human experience: his words, example, his entire life, all have meaning for each of us. Blessed James Alberione prayed, "Master, your life charts the way for me. . . . The manger, Nazareth, Calvary—all indicate the divine way."[14]

As we follow Jesus Master more closely, we discover that he is both the way to the Father and the way to wholeness. Jesus wants to heal our sinfulness and whatever woundedness we carry. He wants us to become free to genuinely love both ourselves and others and to live out our Christian vocation in its deepest sense—as an active presence of God in the world.

It is not easy to be a true follower of Christ, but Jesus assures us that he himself will be with us and that his grace will sustain us. We do not walk alone; Jesus walks alongside us.

Jesus, Life for the World

The foundational belief and experience of Christianity is that Jesus Christ, who is both God and man, is our Redeemer. The Second Person of the Blessed Trinity became man, suffered, died, and rose to save us and bring us into everlasting life. Jesus saves us in countless ways: from original sin, from our personal sins and sinfulness, from social sinfulness, from despair and the evil in the world around us, from the hell of endless separation from God. Ideally, in living our Christian life we experience Jesus' saving love daily in a profoundly personal way.

In saving us, Jesus offers a priceless gift that is unimaginable to the nonbeliever: that is, a sharing in his own life. "I am the vine, you are the branches. Those who abide in me and I in them bear much fruit" (Jn 15:5). Jesus invites us to union with him and to participate in the eternal communion of love of the Most Holy Trinity. That's why the sacraments, beginning with Baptism and preeminently the Eucharist, are such incredible gifts. Through them, we receive and are nourished with the very life of God.

We honor Jesus Life by asking him for the abundance of his life, his grace, his sanctity. In the presence of the magnificent virtue and sanctity that we discover in the life of the Master, we feel the need to resemble him and to pray for his help, and Jesus . . . will grant us the abundance of his Spirit, who will work in us 'until Christ is formed' in us.[15]

To truly live in Christ means not just experiencing the fullness of human life but also really sharing in Jesus' passion, death, and Resurrection. Jesus' self-giving love transforms us so that we can love others in that same selfless way: "Love one another as I have loved you" (Jn 15:12). This call to love often means sacrifice; certainly, it is another way we share in the mystery of Jesus' suffering, death, and Resurrection.

In challenges and suffering, the disciple is consoled and strengthened both by the presence of Jesus and by his promise of resurrection and new life. For the disciple united to Jesus our Life, every form of death can be a mysterious passageway to new life. God does not will evil to happen but rather works through everything—even the most tragic circumstance (like the death of his Only-Begotten Son)—for our good and the good of others.

Jesus lovingly gives himself to us in the Eucharist to share his life with us, and through us, with others. In the Eucharist, Jesus calls us to be his light, his hands, and his heart for our world today.

Part Two

Source and Summit of Our Christian Life

The strength of Jesus' love is irresistible.... Every time I offer Mass, I have the opportunity to extend my hands and nail myself to the cross with Jesus, to drink with him the bitter cup.

—Venerable Francis Xavier Nguyen Van Thuan

The Mass

At the Last Supper, on the night he was betrayed, our Savior instituted the eucharistic sacrifice of his Body and Blood. This he did in order to perpetuate the sacrifice of the Cross throughout the ages until he should come again, and so to entrust to his beloved Spouse, the Church, a memorial of his death and Resurrection: a sacrament of love, a sign of unity, a bond of charity, a paschal banquet "in which Christ is consumed, the mind is filled with grace, and a pledge of future glory is given to us."

—Vatican II[16]

The Eucharist is a mystery of such unfathomable richness and depth that it defies easy description. Even the *Catechism of the Catholic Church* describes the Eucharist with a long list of names, each of which highlight a different aspect of the Mass. Taking the time to reflect on each name one by one could help to reignite our Eucharistic amazement:

Eucharist (from the Greek word meaning thanksgiving)

The Lord's Supper or the Breaking of the Bread

The Eucharistic assembly

The memorial of the Lord's passion and Resurrection

The Holy Sacrifice (also the sacrifice of praise)

The Holy and Divine Liturgy
The Sacred Mysteries
The most Blessed Sacrament
Holy Communion (Bread of Angels, Bread from heaven)
Holy Mass

(For a full list with explanations, see CCC, nos. 1328–1332.)

One way to reflect on the mystery of the Eucharist is to focus on three key aspects often highlighted in the teaching of the Church: the Eucharist as sacrifice, presence, and banquet. Saint John Paul II wrote beautifully about them in his encyclical letter, *Ecclesia de Eucharistia*:

> When the Church celebrates the Eucharist, the memorial of her Lord's death and Resurrection, this central event of salvation becomes really present and "the work of our redemption is carried out." This sacrifice is so decisive for the salvation of the human race that Jesus Christ offered it and returned to the Father only *after he had left us a means of sharing in it* as if we had been present there.[17]
>
> After the consecration... the adorable Body and Blood of the Lord Jesus from that moment on are really before us under the sacramental species of bread and wine.[18]
>
> The Eucharistic Sacrifice is intrinsically directed to the inward union of the faithful with Christ through communion; we receive the very One who offered himself for us, we receive his Body which he gave up for us on the Cross and his Blood which he "poured out for many for the forgiveness of

sins" (Mt 26:28).... The Eucharist is a true banquet, in which Christ offers himself as our nourishment.[19]

Preparing for Mass and Communion

O memorial of the wonders of God's love!
—Saint Katharine Drexel

Routine exposure to even the most awe-inspiring mystery can dull our wonder and reverence. Many Catholics seem to struggle to "get something out of the Mass." How can we approach every Mass as the most incredible act of love for us that we will ever receive?

One way is to prepare well for each Mass so we participate worthily and recognize Jesus' presence and the invitations he wants to give us at *this* Mass. The first way to do this is to receive the Sacrament of Reconciliation regularly (see pages 236–238).

Other ways to ready our minds and hearts to participate at the Eucharistic Celebration are:

- Read and reflect on the Scripture readings ahead of time, either the night before or before Mass (see pages 157–160 for tips for how to pray well with the Bible).
- Arrive early for Mass so that you can have a few moments to greet Jesus in the Blessed Sacrament in

your own words. Make an act of faith in Jesus' Real Presence in the tabernacle.

- When you are at Mass, participate fully. Pay attention to the meaning of the prayers that are being offered and make the sentiments of those prayers your own.
  — In the first part, the Liturgy of the Word, as the lector and the priest read from the Bible, listen for how Jesus may be speaking to you or inviting you into a fuller discipleship and deeper relationship.
  — In the second part, the Liturgy of the Eucharist, place yourself with Mary and the beloved disciple John at the foot of the Cross. Adore Jesus and thank him for his great love for you. Jesus loves you so much that he gave his life for you. This second part of the Mass makes us truly present to the sacrifice Jesus offers to the Father unceasingly on our behalf.
  — In the Communion Rite, prepare your heart to receive Jesus with the prayers that are prayed aloud together, and with your own silent acts of love. After Communion, thank Jesus for coming into your heart, offer him your love, and pray for the intentions you hold most deeply in your heart.

- Stay after Mass—even for just a few minutes—to prolong and deepen your thanksgiving for Jesus' great love for you and his saving action in your life.
- Make acts of spiritual communion throughout the day or week, expressing your longing to be united to Jesus (see page 43).
- Spend time in Eucharistic adoration.

Some of the fruits we can receive at *every* Holy Communion are:

- Union with and transformation in Christ
- Nourishment and strength for the life of the soul
- Purification from venial sins
- Preservation from future mortal sins
- An increase of love
- Comfort and strength to overcome temptations and difficulties
- Growth in unity in the Body of Christ, the Church
- Increased commitment to the those who are poor and suffering
- A pledge of eternal life.

(For a more complete description, see CCC, nos. 1391–1398.)

Blessed James Alberione offers a way of making our participation in the Mass always fresh:

The Sacrifice of the Mass is offered every day, and in substance it is always the same. However, for one devoted to Jesus Christ the Master, Way, Truth, and Life, it always offers some new insight, some new way, some new spiritual comfort.... In the Mass Jesus Christ presents himself to us: in the first part as Truth—the Truth to believe with our whole mind; in the second part as Way and Life—the Way to follow with all our strength, and the Life to whom we unite ourselves with our whole heart.[20]

Prayers Before Mass

> Come, with the staff of faith, approach
> > The mystery senses fail to see;
> Come to this Holy Sacrament,
> > In confidence and certainty;
> For Christ who hides himself therein,
> > His sweet goodwill bestows on thee
> And binds you to this mystery,
> > This grace that he is offering.
>
> JACOPONE DA TODI

Offering of the Holy Mass

> Accept, Most Holy Trinity,
> this Sacrifice fulfilled at one time
> by the divine Word and now renewed
> on this altar through the hands of your priest.
> I unite myself to the intentions of Jesus Christ,
> Priest and Victim,
> that I may be entirely offered for your glory
> and for the salvation of all people.
> Through Jesus Christ,
> with Jesus Christ,
> and in Jesus Christ,
> I intend to adore your eternal majesty,
> to thank your immense goodness,

to satisfy your offended justice,
and to beseech your mercy
for the Church,
for my dear ones,
and for myself.

Blessed James Alberione

A Eucharistic Offertory for the Media

Father, in union with all those celebrating the Eucharist throughout the world, I wish to unite myself with the Heart and intentions of your beloved Son, Jesus, who offered his life for our salvation:

— that the media may always be used to support the good of each person and the common good; to uplift the sacred dignity of every human person, especially those who are poor and most vulnerable; to nurture marriage and family life; to bring about solidarity, peace, greater justice, and equality for all people; and to build respect for the gifts of God's creation;

— in reparation for the errors and scandals spread throughout the world through the misuse of the media;

— to call down your mercy upon those who have been deceived or manipulated by the misuse of the media, and led away from your fatherly love;

— for the conversion of those who have spread error, violence, or a disregard for the dignity of the person by wrongly using the media and rejecting the teaching of Christ and his Church;
— that we may follow Christ alone whom you, Father, in your boundless love, sent into the world, saying, "This is my beloved Son, hear him";
— to acknowledge and to make known that Jesus alone, the Word Incarnate, is the perfect Teacher, the trustworthy Way who leads to knowledge of you, Father, and to a participation in your very life;
— that in the Church the number of priests, religious, and lay people who are dedicated as apostles of the media will increase in number and grow in holiness, making resound throughout the world the message of salvation;
— that all those who work in the media with goodwill (writers, artists, directors, editors, technicians, producers, advertisers, and distributors) may grow in wisdom and uprightness, living and spreading worthy human and Christian values;
— that the undertakings of Catholics in all forms of media may continually increase, so that by more effectively promoting genuine human and Christian values, they will silence the voices that spread error and evil;

— that well aware of our inadequacy and unworthiness, we may recognize our need to draw near the font of life with great humility and trust and be nourished with your Word, Father, and with the Body of Christ, invoking light, love, and mercy for all men and women.

Based on a prayer of Blessed James Alberione

Prayers Before Communion

> Remember . . . that this sweet Jesus is there in the tabernacle expressly for you—for you alone. He burns with the desire to enter your heart.
>
> —Saint Thérèse of Lisieux

Act of Faith, Hope, and Love

Jesus, eternal Truth, I believe you are really present in the signs of bread and wine. You are here with your Body, Blood, soul, and divinity. I hear your invitation: "I am the living bread descended from heaven . . . Take and eat; this is my Body." I believe, Lord and Master, but strengthen my weak faith.

Jesus, sole Way of salvation, you invite me: "Learn from me." But I resemble you so little! Jesus, you pleased the Father; you are my model. Draw me to yourself and give me the grace to imitate you especially in the virtue I need most.

Jesus Master, you assure me: "I am the Life. Whoever eats my flesh and drinks my Blood will have eternal life." In Baptism and in the Sacrament of Reconciliation you have communicated your life to me. Now you nourish it by making yourself my food.

Take my heart; detach it from the vain things of the world. I love you with all my heart, above all things, because you are the supreme good and my eternal happiness.

Blessed James Alberione

Prayer of Saint Ambrose Before Communion

I draw near, loving Lord Jesus Christ,
to the table of your most delightful banquet
in fear and trembling,
a sinner, presuming not upon my own merits,
but trusting rather in your goodness and mercy.
I have a heart and body defiled by my many offences,
a mind and tongue
over which I have kept no good watch.
Therefore, O loving God, O awesome Majesty,
I turn in my misery, caught in snares,
to you the fountain of mercy,
hastening to you for healing,
flying to you for protection;
and while I do not look forward to having you as Judge,
I long to have you as Savior.
To you, O Lord, I display my wounds,
to you I uncover my shame.
I am aware of my many and great sins,
for which I fear,
but I hope in your mercies,
which are without number.
Look upon me, then, with eyes of mercy,
Lord Jesus Christ, eternal King,
God and Man, crucified for mankind.
Listen to me, as I place my hope in you,

Source and Summit of Our Christian Life 37

have pity on me, full of miseries and sins,
you, who will never cease
to let the fountain of compassion flow.
Hail, O Saving Victim,
offered for me and for the whole human race
on the wood of the Cross.
Hail, O noble and precious Blood,
flowing from the wounds
of Jesus Christ, my crucified Lord,
and washing away the sins of all the world.
Remember, Lord, your creature,
whom you redeemed by your Blood.
I am repentant of my sins,
I desire to put right what I have done.
Take from me, therefore, most merciful Father,
all my iniquities and sins,
so that, purified in mind and body,
I may worthily taste the Holy of Holies.
And grant that this sacred foretaste
of your Body and Blood
which I, though unworthy, intend to receive,
may be the remission of my sins,
the perfect cleansing of my faults,
the banishment of shameful thoughts,
and the rebirth of right sentiments; and may it encourage
a wholesome and effective performance
of deeds pleasing to you

and be a most firm defense of body and soul
against the snares of my enemies. Amen.

Saint Ambrose of Milan

Prayer of Love and Humility

Almighty and eternal God, behold I come to the Sacrament of your only-begotten Son, our Lord Jesus Christ. As one sick I come to the physician of life; unclean to the fountain of mercy; blind to the light of eternal splendor; poor and needy to the Lord of heaven and earth. Therefore, I beg you, through your infinite mercy and generosity, heal my weakness, wash my uncleanness, give light to my blindness, enrich my poverty, and clothe me with your grace. May I receive the Bread of Angels, the King of Kings, the Lord of Lords, with such reverence and humility, contrition and devotion, purity and faith, purpose and intention, so as to aid my soul's salvation.

Grant, I beg of you, that I may receive not only the sacrament of the Body and Blood of our Lord, but also its full grace and power. Give me the grace, most merciful God, to receive the Body of your only Son, our Lord Jesus Christ, born of the Virgin Mary, in such a manner that I may deserve to be intimately united with his Mystical Body and to be numbered among his members. Most loving Father, grant that I may behold for all eternity face to face your beloved Son, whom now, on my pilgrimage, I am about to receive under the sacramental veil, who lives and reigns with you, in the unity of the Holy Spirit, God, world without end. Amen.

Saint Thomas Aquinas

Prayer of Gratitude and Faith

I thank you, good Jesus, eternal Shepherd, because you have willed to feed us with your precious Body and Blood, and you invite us to partake of these mysteries by words you yourself said, "Come to me, all you grown weary and burdened, and I will refresh you" (Mt 11:28).

Enlighten my eyes to contemplate this great mystery of the Eucharist and give me strength to believe it with a lively faith. Visit me with your saving grace so that my soul may be nourished by the spiritual sweetness of this Sacrament. May I receive you with devotion, Lord God, and in receiving you, may I be ever more closely united to you.

Thomas à Kempis

Act of Desire

Jesus, my King, my God, and my All, my soul longs for you, my heart yearns to receive you in Holy Communion. Come, Bread of heaven; come, Food of angels, to nourish my soul and to rejoice my heart. Come, most amiable Spouse of my soul, to inflame me with such love of you that I may never again displease you, never again be separated from you by sin. "My soul thirsts for God, for the living God. When shall I come and behold the face of God?" (Ps 42:2) "God is the strength of my heart, and my portion forever" (Ps 72:26).

Come, Lord Jesus

> O Jesus, hidden God, I cry to You,
> O Jesus, hidden Light, I turn to You,
> O Jesus, hidden love, I run to You,
> with all the strength I have, I worship You,
> with all the love I have, I cling to You,
> with all my soul, I long to be with You
> and fear no more to fail or fall from You.
>
> *Henry Augustus Rawes, OSC*

Prayer for Love

O most sweet Lord Jesus, transfix my inmost soul with that most joyous and healthful wound of your love, with true, serene, and holy apostolic charity, that my soul may ever languish and melt with entire love and longing for you, that it may desire you, and faint for your courts, and long to be dissolved and to be with you. Grant that I may hunger after you, the Bread of Angels, the refreshment of holy souls, our daily and supersubstantial Bread, having all sweetness and savor, and the sweetness of every taste. Let my heart ever hunger after and feed upon you who the angels desire to look upon. May my inmost soul be filled with the sweetness of your savor. May I ever thirst for you, the fountain of life, the source of wisdom and knowledge, the fountain of eternal light, the torrent of pleasure, the richness of the house of God. May I ever yearn for you, seek you, find you, stretch toward you, attain to you, meditate upon you, speak of you, and do all things to the praise and glory of your holy name, with humility and discretion, with love and delight, with readiness and affection, with perseverance until death. May you ever be my hope, and my whole confidence; my riches; my delight; my pleasure and my joy; my rest and tranquility; my peace, my sweetness, and my fragrance; my sweet savor, my food and refreshment; my refuge and my help; my wisdom; my portion, my possession, and my treasure, in whom my mind and my heart may ever remain fixed and firm, and rooted immovably, henceforth and forevermore. Amen.

Saint Bonaventure

Act of Love and Desire

Oh, that I could love you, Jesus, as if I had knelt at your feet and felt the touch of your hand on my brow and heard your gentle voice that uttered absolutions and gave encouragement to the sick and the unfortunate. Oh, that I could love you, as the poor of Galilee loved you, as Mary Magdalen loved you, as

Saint Peter and Saint John, the beloved disciple, loved you, as she, who knew you best—your Blessed Mother—loved you, and, most of all, O Lord, as you have loved me.

Let me at least love you with all my heart and soul and mind and strength. And let my love be worthy of the name—showing itself by confidence, by generosity, by sacrifice—acknowledging cheerfully that all that you permit is best for me and counting no cost when I work for you—giving up gladly what is dear to me when you ask it, when it will help to serve you better and to further the interests of your Sacred Heart.

Dispose of me, O Lord, as it pleases you; for from henceforth I am entirely yours. I offer you all that I am and all that I have. I will labor and suffer for your glory, for the salvation of others, and for my own sanctification.

Come, my Jesus, crucified for love of me. Come, dear Jesus, in the Sacrament of your love, and be all mine, as I desire to be all yours. O Blessed Virgin, my tender Mother, who obtained from your divine Son a wonderful miracle at the wedding feast at Cana, see my misery and the need I have of your assistance; obtain for me from Jesus a prodigy of his almighty power, that my coldness and tepidity may be changed into ardent charity. Amen.

Eucharistic Offering

"Lord, all that is in the heavens and on the earth is yours" (1 Chr 29:11).

I want to offer myself freely to you as a sacrifice and remain always yours.

Today, Lord, in the simplicity of my heart, I offer myself to you as a servant forever, as a gift and a sacrifice of eternal praise.

Receive me together with this holy oblation of your precious Body, which I offer to you this day in the presence of your angels, who are your invisible assistants, so it may bring salvation to me and all people.

Thomas à Kempis

Act of Spiritual Communion

If for some reason you are unable to receive Holy Communion, you can make a spiritual communion with a prayer such as this:

My Jesus, I believe that you are truly present in the Blessed Sacrament. Thank you for this wonderful gift. I love you above all things and I desire you in my soul. Please forgive my sins and failings, for which I am deeply sorry. As I cannot now receive you sacramentally, come at least spiritually into my heart. I embrace you and unite myself entirely to you.

Prayers After Communion

> The greatest love story of all time is contained in a tiny white Host.
>
> —Attributed to Venerable Fulton J. Sheen

Act of Adoration

I adore you present in me, Incarnate Word,
only-begotten Son and splendor of the Father,
    born of Mary.
I thank you, sole Master and Truth,
for having deigned to come to me, ignorant
    and sinful as I am.
With Mary I offer you to the Father:
through you, with you, in you,
may there be eternal praise,
thanksgiving, and supplication
for peace to all people.
Enlighten my mind;
grant that I may be a faithful disciple of the Church;
let me live a life of faith;
give me an understanding of the Scriptures,
make me your ardent apostle.
Let the light of your Gospel
shine to the farthest bounds of the world.

Blessed James Alberione

Act of Resolution

Jesus, you are the Way I want to follow;
the perfect model that I must imitate.
When I come before you at the judgment
I want to be found similar to you.
O divine model of humility and obedience,
make me similar to you.
You who loved without limit and with a pure heart,
make me similar to you.
O Jesus, poor and patient,
make me similar to you.
You who loved everyone and sought to bring everyone
   to your Father,
make me similar to you.

Blessed James Alberione

Act of Supplication

Jesus, my Life, my joy and source of all good,
I love you. Above all, I ask of you
that I may love you more and more
and all those redeemed by your Blood.
You are the vine, and I am the branch:
I want to remain always united to you
   so as to bear much fruit.
You are the source:
pour out an ever greater abundance of grace

to sanctify my soul.
You are my head, I, your member:
communicate to me your Holy Spirit
with the Spirit's gifts.
May your kingdom come through Mary.
Console and save all my dear ones.
Bring those who have died into your presence.
Assist all who share your mission of spreading
    the Good News.
Bless the Church with many vocations
to the priesthood and religious life. Amen.

Blessed James Alberione

Thanksgiving for the Gift of the Eucharist

I thank you, Lord, almighty Father, everlasting God, for having been pleased, through no merit of mine, but of your great mercy alone, to feed me, a sinner and your unworthy servant, with the precious Body and Blood of your Son, our Lord Jesus Christ. I pray that this Holy Communion may not be for my judgment and condemnation, but for my pardon and salvation. Let this Holy Communion be for me an armor of faith and a shield of goodwill, a cleansing of all vices, and a purging of all evil desires. May it increase love, patience, humility, obedience, and all virtues. May it be a defense against the designs of the evil one, and a perfect quieting of all distorted desires of soul and body. May this Holy Communion bring about a perfect union with you, the one true God, and at last enable me to reach eternal bliss when you call me to yourself. I pray that you bring me, a sinner, to the heavenly banquet where you, with your Son, Jesus Christ, and the Holy Spirit, are true light, full blessedness, everlasting joy, and perfect happiness. Amen.

Saint Thomas Aquinas

Act of Thanksgiving

My dear Jesus, I thank you with all my heart for coming to me and nourishing my soul with your sacred Body and most precious Blood. I thank you for all the graces and blessings I have ever received through the merits of your sacred passion and through the institution of the most holy Sacrament of the altar. With the help of your grace, I will endeavor to manifest my gratitude to you by greater devotion to you in the sacrament of your love, by obedience to your holy commandments, by fidelity to my duties, by kindness to my neighbor, and by an earnest endeavor to become more like you in my daily behavior. Blessed be your holy name!

I Will Remain with You...

> This Heart, it beats for us in a small tabernacle
> Where it remains mysteriously hidden
> In that still, white Host.

That is your royal throne on earth, O Lord,
Which visibly you have erected for us,
And you are pleased when I approach it.

Full of love, you sink your gaze into mine
And bend your ear to my quiet words
And deeply fill my heart with peace.

Yet your love is not satisfied
With this exchange that could still lead to separation:
Your Heart requires more.

You come to me as early morning's meal each daybreak.
Your flesh and Blood become food and drink for me
And something wonderful happens.

Your Body mysteriously permeates mine
And your soul unites with mine:
I am no longer what once I was.

Excerpt, Saint Teresa Benedicta of the Cross[21]

To Jesus Crucified

See page 235.

Prayer for Perseverance

Good Jesus, my dear Lord and Master, what strength you have given my soul in this sacred banquet! But how much I need this grace! Keep me in your love; keep me in your grace to the end of my life. The road I travel is so difficult, that without you I should fear to venture upon it. When I go about my daily occupations, I am exposed to the same temptations and find myself with my usual faults. But Jesus, you who helped the saints, come to me. Stay with me, and by your grace help me to speak and act with all modesty, meekness, and humility. Help me to make your presence visible to all; let others see your love and kindness shining through me. Amen.

I Am Not Worthy

O Lord my God, I am not worthy that you should enter my soul; but as you desire, according to your loving kindness, to dwell in me, I venture to draw near to you. You ask me to open the gates of my soul, which you have made, that you may enter with your loving kindness and enlighten my darkened mind. I believe you will do this, for you did not cast away the sinful woman who came to you in tears, nor did you reject the repentant sinner, nor the thief on the Cross who acknowledged your kingdom, nor did you leave Paul, the repentant persecutor, to himself. Lord, you include all who come to you in repentance among your friends, O you who alone are blessed, always, now, and to everlasting ages. Amen.

Saint John Chrysostom

Soul of Christ

Soul of Christ, sanctify me.
Body of Christ, save me.
Blood of Christ, inebriate me.
Water from the side of Christ, wash me.
Passion of Christ, strengthen me.
Good Jesus, hear me.
Within your wounds hide me.
Never let me be parted from thee.
From the evil one protect me.
In the hour of my death, call me
and bid me come to thee,
that with thy saints I may praise thee
forever and ever. Amen.

Anima Christi

Anima Christi, sanctífica me;
Corpus Christi, salva me;
Sanguis Christi, inébria me;
Aqua láteris Christi, lava me;
Pássio Christi, confórta me;
O bone Jesu, exáudi me.
Intra vúlnera tua, abscónde me;
Ne permíttas me separári a te;
Ab hoste maligno defénde me;
In hora mortis meae voca me;
Et iube me veníre ad te;
Ut cum sanctis tuis laudem te.
Per infinita saécula sæculórum. Amen.

Acts of Adoration, Thanksgiving, Reparation, and Prayer

Jesus, my Lord and my God! I adore you. With Magdalen I kiss your sacred feet. With John, the beloved disciple, let me rest upon your Sacred Heart. I love you and desire to love you more and more. Speak to me and tell me what you desire me to do. I am your servant, ready to do your will. Establish your kingdom firmly in my heart; remove all my self-love and pride. I give you thanks, O Lord, for condescending in your goodness and love to give yourself to one who is so poor and miserable, so imperfect and unfaithful.

Mary, my Queen, my mother, and all you angels and saints of heaven, thank the Lord for me; praise him for his goodness; bless him for his mercy.

My God! I am truly sorry for having offended you so often and so grievously. I will strive to make reparation for my past ingratitude by my fidelity to your grace, by my devotedness to my duties, by seeking to please you perfectly in all my actions, and by honoring you especially in the Holy Eucharist. I resolve to fight against that sin that causes me to fall the most often and to resist every evil inclination of my heart. For love of you I will also be kind to others in thought, word, and deed.

Bless me, Lord. Keep me in your love. Grant me the grace of perseverance.

Sweet Heart of Jesus, may I love you more and more. Jesus, meek and humble of heart, make my heart like unto yours. May your holy will, O God, be done in me and through me now and forever.

Litany of Holy Communion

This litany may be prayed before or after Communion.

Lord, have mercy on us. *Christ, have mercy on us.*

Lord, have mercy on us. Christ, hear us. *Christ, graciously hear us.*

God, the Father of heaven, ℟. *have mercy on us.*

God, the Son, Redeemer of the world, ℟.

God, the Holy Spirit, ℟.

Holy Trinity, one God, ℟.

Jesus, Living Bread come down from heaven, ℟.

Jesus, Bread from heaven giving life to the world, ℟.

Hidden God and Savior, ℟.

My Lord and my God, ℟.

Who loved us with an everlasting love, ℟.

Whose delight is to be with the children of men, ℟.

Who gave your flesh for the life of the world, ℟.

Who invite all to come to you, ℟.

Who promise eternal life to those who receive you, ℟.

Who desired to eat the Pasch with us, ℟.

Who are ever ready to receive and welcome us, ℟.

Who stand at our door knocking, ℟.

Who said that if we open the door to you,
 you will come in and sup with us, ℟.

Who receive us into your arms and bless us
 with the little children, ℟.

Who allow us to sit at your feet with Magdalen, ℟.

Who invite us to lean on your bosom with
 the beloved disciple, ℟.

Who did not leave us orphans, ℟.

Most dear Sacrament, ℟.

Sacrament of love, ℟.

Sacrament of sweetness, ℟.

Life-giving Sacrament, ℟.

Sacrament of strength, ℟.

My God and my All, ℟.

That our hearts may long for you as the deer
 for springs of water, ℟.

That you would manifest yourself to us as to
 the two disciples in the breaking of bread, ℟.

That we may recognize your voice like Magdalen, ℟.

That with lively faith we may confess with
 the beloved disciple: "It is the Lord," ℟.

Source and Summit of Our Christian Life

That you would bless us who have
    not seen and have believed, ℟. *we beseech you, hear us.*

That we may love you in the Blessed Sacrament
    with our whole heart, with our whole soul,
    with all our mind, and with all our strength, ℟.

That the fruit of each Communion may be renewed love, ℟.

That our one desire may be to love you and to
    do your will, ℟.

That we may ever remain in your love, ℟.

That you would teach us how to receive
    and welcome you, ℟.

That you would teach us to pray, and yourself
    pray within us, ℟.

That with you every virtue may come into our souls, ℟.

That throughout this day you would keep us
    closely united to you, ℟.

That you would give us grace to persevere to the end, ℟.

That you would then be our support and Viaticum, ℟.

That with you and leaning on you we may safely pass
    through all dangers, ℟.

That our last act may be one of perfect love, and
    our last breath a long, deep sigh to be in
    our Father's house, ℟.

That your sweet face may smile upon us when we
> appear before you, ℟.

That our separation from you, dearest Lord,
> may not be very long, ℟.

That when the time is come, we may fly from
> our purification to you and in your Sacred Heart
> find our rest forever, ℟.

> Lamb of God, who take away the sins of the world:
> *spare us, O Lord.*
> Lamb of God, who take away the sins of the world:
> *graciously hear us.*
> Lamb of God, who take away the sins of the world:
> *have mercy on us.*

℣. Stay with us, Lord, because it is toward evening:
℟. And the day is far spent.

Let us pray.

We come to you, dear Lord, with the apostles, saying: Increase our faith. Give us a strong and lively faith in the mystery of your Real Presence in the midst of us. Give us the splendid faith of the centurion, which drew from you such praise. Give us the faith of the beloved disciple, to know you even in the dark and say: It is the Lord. Give us the faith of Martha to confess: You are Christ, the Son of the living God.

Give us the faith of Magdalen to fall at your feet crying: Rabboni, Master! Give us the faith of all your saints, who understood the Blessed Sacrament as heaven begun on earth. In every Communion increase our faith and fill us with love, humility, and reverence and all goodwill. Amen.

Mother Mary Loyola

Benediction

I put before you
the one great thing
to love on earth:
the Blessed Sacrament.
There you will find romance,
glory, honor, fidelity,
and the true way
of all your loves upon earth,
and more than that.

— J. R. R. Tolkien[22]

Because Christ himself is present in the Sacrament of the altar, he is to be honored with the worship of adoration (see CCC no. 1378). Adoration can be brief or long or even extended throughout the day with adorers taking turns before the Blessed Sacrament.

Often adoration begins with exposition: The sacred Host is removed from the tabernacle by a priest, deacon, or designated minister and placed in a monstrance, then set upon the altar for all to see and worship. The minister incenses the Host, and a hymn honoring Jesus in the Eucharist is sung.

Benediction comes at the close of adoration: The celebrant again kneels before the altar and incenses the most Blessed Sacrament. The "Tantum Ergo" or another hymn of Eucharistic adoration is sung. The celebrant prays and the people respond. He then blesses the people with the sacred Host. The Divine Praises are recited together, and the Blessed Sacrament is returned to the tabernacle, while those present sing a hymn of Eucharistic praise.

O Saving Victim

> O saving Victim, opening wide,
> The gate of heaven to man below!
> Our foes press on from every side;
> Thine aid supply, thy strength bestow.
>
> To Thy great name be endless praise,
> Immortal Godhead, one in Three;
> Oh, grant us endless length of days,
> In our true native land with thee. Amen.

O Salutaris Hostia

O salutaris Hostia
Quae coeli pandis ostium!
Bella premunt hostilia,
Da robur, fer auxilium!

Uni trinoque Domino
Sit sempiterna gloria,
Qui vitam sine termino
Nobis donet in patria. Amen.

Saint Thomas Aquinas

Humbly Let Us Voice Our Homage

> Humbly let us voice our homage
> for so great a sacrament:
> let all former rites surrender
> to the Lord's new Testament;
> what our senses fail to fathom
> let us grasp through faith's consent!
>
> Glory, honor, adoration
> let us sing with one accord!
> Praised be God, almighty Father;
> praised be Christ, his Son, our Lord;
> praised be God, the Holy Spirit;
> Triune Godhead be adored! Amen.

The following verse and response may be added:

℣. You have given them bread from heaven (alleluia).
℟. Having all sweetness within it (alleluia).

Let us pray.

O God, who in this wonderful Sacrament have left us a memorial of your Passion, grant us, we pray, so to revere the sacred mysteries of your Body and Blood that we may always experience in ourselves the fruits of your redemption. Who live and reign forever and ever. Amen.

Tantum Ergo

Tantum ergo sacraméntum
Venerémur cérnui:
Et antíquum documéntum
Novo cedat rítui:
Praestet fides suppleméntum
Sénsuum deféctui.

Genitóri, Genitóque
Laus et jubilátio,
Salus, honor, virtus quoque
Sit et benedíctio:
Procedénti ab utróque
Compar sit laudátio. Amen.

℣. Panem de cælo præstitísti eis (alleluia).
℟. Omne delectaméntum in se habéntem (alleluia).

Orémus.

Deus, qui nobis sub sacraménto mirábili, passiónis tuæ memóriam reliquísti: tríbue, quæsumus, ita nos córporis et sánguinis tui sacra mystéria venerári, ut redemptiónis tuæ fructum in nobis iúgiter sentiámus. Qui vivis et regnas cum Deo Patre in unitáte Spíritus Sancti Deus, in sæcula sæculórum. Amen.

Saint Thomas Aquinas

After Benediction

The Divine Praises

>Blessed be God.
>Blessed be his holy name.
>Blessed be Jesus Christ, true God and true man.
>Blessed be the name of Jesus.
>Blessed be his most Sacred Heart.
>Blessed be his most precious Blood.
>Blessed be Jesus in the most Holy Sacrament of the altar.
>Blessed be the Holy Spirit, the Paraclete.
>Blessed be the great Mother of God, Mary most holy.
>Blessed be her holy and Immaculate Conception.
>Blessed be her glorious Assumption.
>Blessed be the name of Mary, Virgin and Mother.
>Blessed be Saint Joseph, her most chaste spouse.
>Blessed be God in his angels and in his saints.

How to Live a Eucharistic Day

> To walk with the Divine Friend who knows how to console those who seek him and confide in him is a great source of comfort. The Eucharistic day is the most effective way of sanctifying one's day. It is to feel in a practical way how Jesus Christ is truly Way, Truth, and Life.
>
> —Blessed James Alberione[23]

Jesus gives himself in the Holy Eucharist first of all for us individually and personally: for our joy and salvation, but not for us alone. He comes to us also for the sake of others: for our loved ones, for everyone we know and meet, and for those whose lives we unknowingly touch. Eucharistic spirituality involves much more than times of prayer, as important as those are. At every encounter with Jesus in the Eucharist, we are changed to be a little more like Jesus. Jesus gives us his light, love, examples, and invitations to transform us and draw us more fully into the paschal mystery.

While we receive many graces simply by approaching Jesus in the Blessed Sacrament, we can deepen our receptivity by trying to soften any resistance we might have and open our hearts to fully receive the love, light, and healing Jesus brings us. We can do this by bringing our whole self to every Eucharistic encounter with Jesus.

Jesus wants to transform us. Jesus wants us to become *his* presence and love in the world. We are to become Eucharistic reflections, loving others as Jesus would.

Several saints, including Blessed James Alberione and Saint Peter Julian Eymard, recommend centering our whole day around the most Holy Eucharist as a spiritual practice that can help us to live eucharistically. Intentionally centering each day around the Eucharist will help us to center our entire life around Jesus.

Some Practical Tips for Living a Eucharistic Day

Begin your day with a morning offering that unites you and your whole day to Jesus' offering of himself to the Father in the Holy Mass (see page 31).

If you can go to daily Mass in the morning, divide the day into two parts:

1. Spend your morning thanking and glorifying God for the great gift of his saving love renewed every day on the altar at Holy Mass, and for the awesome privilege of receiving Jesus in Holy Communion.

2. From noon to night, unite your heart to Jesus in the Eucharist and with him, offer everything to God. Direct all your intentions and actions as acts of love to ready your heart to participate at Mass and to receive Jesus in Holy Communion on the following day.

When you go weekly to Sunday Mass, unite yourself during your daily morning prayer to the Masses being celebrated throughout the world. Renew this offering again before retiring at night.

Regardless of whether you go to daily Mass or are only able to participate in Sunday Mass, try to visit the Blessed Sacrament during the week: Make a weekly hour of adoration whenever possible. Whenever you can, stop to visit a church or adoration chapel—if possible, daily or a couple of times a week. Even a quick visit to Jesus in the Blessed Sacrament can bear abundant fruit in our lives.

Any day you are unable to go to Mass, take some quiet time that day to read and pray with the Bible, especially from the Gospels. At the end of your prayer with the word of God, make a spiritual communion—an act of love for and desire to be united with Jesus in the Holy Eucharist.

Whenever you experience a challenge, difficulty, or suffering, make a spiritual "visit" to Jesus in the tabernacle, renewing your act of love and offering your difficulty or suffering to him as a form of prayer.

Conclude your night prayers with an act of adoration for Jesus in all the tabernacles of the world, especially where he is alone.

Part Three

Holy Hour Guides

You will learn to integrate yourself, pull yourself together ... precisely in proportion as you manage to get more closely and more intimately in touch with the Eucharistic life of our Blessed Lord. The Blessed Sacrament is the Sacrament of unity; and when you receive it, it does not merely produce in you more charity towards your neighbor, more loyalty towards the Church, more unselfishness in your human attachments, but makes you more at unity with yourself; it catches up your life into a rhythm that echoes the heavenly music.... It comes to you ... full of that unifying love which is the bond of the Blessed Trinity.

—Ronald Knox

The guides offered here are designed according to the Pauline spirituality: a simple, Christ-centered, and Scripture-based plan for Eucharistic hours of adoration that is valuable for both the beginner and the experienced. Blessed James Alberione's integrative and holistic approach to spirituality not only spurs us on to live our call to holiness: "For to me, living is Christ" (Phil 1:21). It also urges us to integrate every aspect of our lives into our relationship with Christ, challenging our tendency to live a fragmented life, even the woundedness that we may hide from others, due to embarrassment or shame. In the face of the fragmentation that many people experience in their lives today, Alberione's spirituality is a welcome invitation to integration, wholeness, and holiness. The Eucharistic Jesus invites us to drop our masks in front of him and, in the light of his love, to come to appreciate and respect our deepest, truest selves. Secure in his love, we can open ourselves to the transforming power of his grace in all areas of our lives. Then we can gradually become ever more faithful instruments of his love for transforming the world.

The Pauline Hour of Adoration

Realize that you may gain more in a quarter of an hour of prayer before the Blessed Sacrament than in all the other spiritual practices of the day.

—Saint Alphonsus de Liguori

The simple structure of the Pauline hour of adoration is divided into three "moments" or parts, based on the threefold description Jesus gives of himself as Way, Truth, and Life. In the first part, or "moment," we adore Jesus, listening attentively to his word to us today and letting his Truth shape our minds and attitudes. In the second moment, we contemplate Jesus as our Way and model, looking at our own lives in the light of his loving presence. In the third moment, we open our hearts to Jesus Life to let his sustaining grace and peace fill our hearts so that we can bring that same peace and love to others.

How to Make a Pauline Hour of Adoration

Begin by becoming attentive to the presence of God. Choose a hymn or a prayer, a particular intention to pray for, or a theme to pray with. Slow your mind, seeking to focus your attention on this precious time with Christ.

1. Adoring Jesus Truth

We adore Jesus in his word, opening ourselves to his light and the gift of faith.

Ask the Holy Spirit to enlighten you.

Read a passage of Scripture you have chosen, or perhaps the upcoming Sunday's Gospel reading at Mass, and adore Jesus in his word. Listen attentively with your mind and heart, opening yourself to Jesus Truth and whatever insight he wants to give you. Reread the passage, reflect on what it means for you, and converse with Jesus about how his word touches your life.

Conclude this first part by responding with an act of faith, affirming both your belief in and commitment to Christ.

Tip: Adoring Jesus Truth through frequent reading of the Scriptures will strengthen your faith and influence your attitudes. You will gradually begin to see and experience life more in the light of faith—a faith that will transform your thoughts and mentality into "the mind of Christ" (see Phil 2:5).

You may find that reading a very brief passage gives you a great deal to reflect on, but if not, it might be useful to read more until something sparks an insight. However, it is more important to take time for reflection and conversation with Jesus rather than simply reading.

2. Following Jesus Way

Taking up the theme of the Scripture passage, reflect on God's action in your own life, contemplating Jesus as your Way and model.

Looking over your life (the past month, week, or day), reflect on and thank God for the many and marvelous ways he has blessed you and been at work in your life.

After your thanksgiving, consider how you have responded to the gifts God has given you, asking yourself questions such as:

- How is Jesus calling me to follow him more closely?
- How do I need to change—in my attitudes, actions, thoughts, or desires—so that I can become more like Christ?

Try to imagine what Jesus would do in your place, and how you can draw closer to the Father. Then express sorrow for your sins and renew your resolve to more faithfully follow Christ in the concrete way you live your life. Conclude with a prayer of trust that Jesus will give you the graces you need to be his presence in the world today.

Tip: Both thanksgiving and examining your life are important to this time of prayer. Without an appreciation of God's goodness to you, it is easy to become self-centered or discouraged. Without recognizing your weaknesses, your gratitude could become very superficial. God loves you in your weaknesses, not despite them. In this second part, open yourself to living in continual conversion.

3. In Union with Jesus Life

Seek to grow in your union with Jesus through prayers of intercession and heart-to-heart conversation with Christ.

Converted anew, seek to enter into more intimate communication with Jesus as your Life, the source of grace, strength, and union with the Father. United to Jesus Life, contemplate his love for the Father, for all humanity, and for each person. Bring to God both your own needs and those of the world. Prayers of petition and intercession, as well as prayers of praise and contemplation of God's goodness, may rise from your heart. You might pray in your own words in familiar conversation with Jesus, or you might pray the Rosary, the Stations of the Cross, the Liturgy of the Hours, a psalm, a chaplet, a litany, or other favorite prayers. Offer Jesus your heart in love to become completely one with him and to be transformed in him for the sake of others.

Tip: This third part is time for "prayer of the heart," that is, letting yourself be loved by the Lord, sharing with God your needs, your deepest desires, and the needs of others, and asking to be transformed into a witness of his love and truth.

Sent Forth

Conclude your hour of adoration with an act of love, intentionally taking with you the insights, gratitude, and graces you have pondered and received. True prayer never simply leaves you in the comfort of a quiet chapel or the complacency of a self-centered life but compels you to live the Gospel fully in your own life. As you come to know, love, and follow Jesus Master, Way, Truth, and Life, seek to respond to his invitation to become like him way, truth, and life for our world today.

Practical Notes

Times of adoration are meant to be intensely personal moments spent with our loving Master. The hours of adoration offered here flow from the rich tradition of Pauline spirituality, but are intended to be used freely, as outlines and suggestions, according to the invitations of the Holy Spirit. They are intended to inspire your prayer; simply reading one through without personal reflection and conversation with Jesus will not last a full hour. Adapt each hour as is helpful for you. A rigid division between the three parts is not important; what is essential is to spend some time with each of these three moments. Eventually, you will confidently adapt the Pauline method to spontaneously make your own hours of adoration. The variety of prayers and Scripture passages will help you do just that.

The more we glimpse the face of Christ in Eucharistic prayer, the more we recognize his urgent call to be his loving presence in the world today, especially by loving service to those who suffer from brokenness, poverty, injustice, oppression, alienation, loneliness, or illness. The more we witness to Christ, the greater our need to be nurtured by him in the Eucharist.

Holy Hour One

Encountering the Master

Rediscovering who Jesus is for you at this moment in your life.

Prayer of Awareness

Lord, it is good to be here in your Eucharistic presence, to adore you, to be able to spend some privileged, intimate moments with you. I want to be fully present to you and treasure this time with you.

Lord, I love you. I want to know you better, as good friends desire to know each other always more. Knowing you better, I will love you more. I can never love you enough. Help me to discover what you would like our relationship to become.

Reveal yourself to me and help me to be open and attentive to what you want to say to me in your word today.

Spend a few moments in silent adoration.

Adoring Jesus Truth

Ask the light of the Holy Spirit to illumine your mind and heart. In today's reading, Jesus asks the disciples to tell him what they think of him. Is Jesus inviting you to a heart-to-heart conversation about your relationship with him? Read the following passage of Scripture slowly, pausing to ponder what impresses you.

Reading: Matthew 16:13–19

> Now when Jesus came into the district of Caesarea Philippi, he asked his disciples, "Who do people say that the Son of Man is?" And they said, "Some say John the Baptist, but others Elijah, and still others Jeremiah or one of the prophets." He said to them, "But who do you say that I am?" Simon Peter answered, "You are the Messiah, the Son of the living God." And Jesus answered him, "Blessed are you, Simon son of Jonah! For flesh and blood has not revealed this to you, but my Father in heaven. And I tell you, you are Peter, and on this rock I will build my church, and the gates of Hades will not prevail against it. I will give you the keys of the kingdom of heaven, and whatever you bind on earth will be bound in heaven, and whatever you loose on earth will be loosed in heaven."

Reflection

"Who do you say I am?" Let this direct question of Jesus penetrate your heart. Who is Jesus for you today? Jesus constantly reveals himself to us in the Scriptures, in the Eucharist, in our daily lives. Take a few moments to think about your relationship with Jesus. By what name do you usually call Jesus? What name of his is most meaningful to you?

Holy Hour Guides 79

After some moments of reflection, pray the Litany to Jesus Master as an act of faith in response to the reading, adding your own favorite title of Jesus at the end.

Litany to Jesus Master

Jesus Master—Way, Truth, and Life, ℟. *have mercy on me!*
Jesus, gentle master, ℟. *increase my faith!*
Jesus Truth, light of the world, ℟.
Jesus, Word of the Father, ℟.
Jesus, fulfillment of all my dreams, ℟.
Jesus, light of my life, ℟.
Jesus, salt of my life, ℟.
Jesus, center of my life, ℟.
Jesus, mystery of love, ℟.
Jesus, who knows my inmost thoughts, ℟.
Jesus, present in the tabernacle, ℟.
Jesus, revealer of the Father's love, ℟.
Jesus, who gives meaning to every event in my life, ℟.
Jesus, my inspiration, ℟.
Jesus, God beyond my imagination, ℟.
Jesus, Way to the Father, ℟. *I trust in you.*
Jesus, my guide, ℟.
Jesus, Way for the lost, ℟.
Jesus, model of holiness, ℟.

Jesus, companion on the journey, ℟.

Jesus, my security, ℟.

Jesus Master, who counts all my tears as precious, ℟.

Jesus, my rock and refuge, ℟.

Jesus, my unfailing hope, ℟.

Jesus always with me, ℟.

Jesus, partner in the dance of life, ℟.

Jesus, faithful friend, ℟.

Jesus, who shapes and molds me through life's daily situations, ℟.

Jesus, on whom I lean, ℟.

Jesus, Good Shepherd, ℟.

Jesus, joy of my life, ℟. *live in me.*

Jesus, unconditional lover, ℟.

Jesus, life-giving Bread, ℟.

Jesus, ever-flowing water, ℟.

Jesus, my all, ℟.

Jesus, my Redeemer, ℟.

Jesus, my deepest desire, ℟.

Jesus, who died for me, ℟.

Jesus, healing Master, ℟.

Jesus, transformer of hearts, ℟.

Jesus, my beloved, ℟.

Jesus, gentle listener, ℟.

Jesus, faithful beyond death, ℟.

Jesus, suffering with your people, ℟.

Jesus, my delight, ℟.

Jesus, who calls me, ℟. *have mercy on me!*

Jesus, who molds me, ℟.

Jesus, who challenges me, ℟.

Jesus, who sends me, ℟.

Jesus Master—Way, Truth, and Life, ℟.

Following Jesus Way

In the Scripture reading from Matthew, Jesus gives Simon a new name: Peter. You were given a "new" name when you were baptized, symbolizing your new relationship with God. Jesus continues to call you by name each day, inviting you into a deeper relationship with him, on a "first name" basis. Does Jesus call you by your given name? A special name? How does your name affirm Jesus' great love for you and how precious you are to him?

Every time you go to Mass and receive Communion, Jesus lovingly offers himself to you. Saint Teresa de Los Andes wrote,

> Jesus is present and lives in our midst in the Eucharist. Let us listen to him, for he is Truth. Let us look at him, for he is the face of the Father. Let us love him, for he is love giving himself to his creatures. He comes to our soul so that it may

disappear in him and become divine. What union, however great, can compare to this?[24]

Have you felt the presence of Jesus very close to you? Faith tells us that he is closer to us than we are to ourselves. Take a few moments to thank the Lord for the incredible gift of his relationship with you, especially for the gift of his love in the Holy Eucharist.

After a suitable time of thanksgiving in your own words, unite your thanksgiving with that of Mary by praying the Magnificat on page 178.

In listening to the Master's words and reflecting on Jesus' great love for you, have you heard Jesus inviting you to follow him more closely? Saint Thérèse of Lisieux reminds us, "Jesus wants to possess your heart completely. He wants you to be a great saint."[25] Perhaps you see some ways in which you have not responded to Christ's love for you—a love always present and at work in your life, even when you can't see or don't understand it.

Pause now to bring to Jesus those situations in your life in which you find it difficult to hear or follow his call: the challenges to holiness you face in your life. Reflect on how you handled those challenges and compare your words and actions with the words and example of Jesus.

Express your sorrow and trust in the Lord with an act of contrition.

My loving God, with all my heart I am sorry
for the times I acted out of malice or weakness,
or when I failed to act out of love.
Have mercy on me and forgive me,
in the name of your Son, Jesus, who died for us.
Strengthen me and help me to avoid all sin.
With your grace, I will try to always live in your love.

Sharing Jesus' Life

The Scriptures, especially the psalms, are filled with images of God—God is rock, inheritance, strength, maker, builder, and shepherd. Choose one of your favorite psalms or a psalm included in the Treasury of Prayers, pages 161–174, or make up a psalm of your own to praise God for drawing you into relationship with him. Using the words of the psalm, take some time to savor the gift of your relationship with Jesus and how that affects the world.

As a concluding prayer, pray this contemporary psalm to the Divine Master.

The Lord is my Master,
he teaches me how to love.
Most patient, he understands
the inner movements of my soul.
The Lord lights up my darkness.
Through all creation, he teaches me—

I will sit forever at his feet.
He speaks softly within me,
leading my heart.
Though I can't see the path,
his eyes never lose me.
Turning to him I am safe,
enfolded in his Love.
He calls me to follow him more closely—
clasping his nail-pierced hand.
My Master died and rose for me,
loving me into life.
He transforms every sadness.
His ever-present kindness and mercy
make each day shine anew.
I sing out my joy in him
and proclaim his abundant goodness.
He fills up my life.

Inspired by Psalm 23

As you prepare to leave Jesus' Eucharistic presence, make a spiritual communion (see page 43) and choose one way you can share with someone else the gift that your relationship with Jesus has been for you.

Holy Hour Two
Bread of Life

*Growing in love for Jesus in the Eucharist and
in imitation of his selfless love for all humanity.*

The Eucharist is Jesus' gift of himself to you. He helps you to recognize his presence in your own situation, in your needs, in every aspect of your life. God wants to give you abundant life and to live in ever deeper communion with you. During this time of adoration, pray for the grace to better prepare for and receive Jesus in every Holy Communion.

We begin by adoring Jesus the Divine Master present among us in the Eucharist.

Act of Faith in Jesus' Eucharistic Presence

Jesus, eternal Truth, I believe you are really present in the Eucharist. You are here with your Body, Blood, soul, and divinity. I hear your invitation: "I am the living Bread come down from heaven. Take and eat; this is my Body." I believe, O Lord and Master, but increase my faith.

Blessed James Alberione

Adoring Jesus Truth

The miraculous story of the feeding of thousands with just a few loaves and a couple of fish is recounted in all four Gospels because it was such an important event for the first Christians. As we read it now, we ask the Holy Spirit to be with us and help us discover how this story is important for us today.

READING: JOHN 6:1–15

After this Jesus went to the other side of the Sea of Galilee, also called the Sea of Tiberias. A large crowd kept following him, because they saw the signs that he was doing for the sick. Jesus went up the mountain and sat down there with his disciples. Now the Passover, the festival of the Jews, was near. When he looked up and saw a large crowd coming toward him, Jesus said to Philip, "Where are we to buy bread for these people to eat?" He said this to test him, for he himself knew what he was going to do. Philip answered him, "Six months' wages would not buy enough bread for each of them to get a little." One of his disciples, Andrew, Simon Peter's brother, said to him, "There is a boy here who has five barley loaves and two fish. But what are they among so many people?" Jesus said, "Make the people sit down." Now there was a great deal of grass in the place; so they sat down, about five thousand in all. Then Jesus took the loaves, and when he had given thanks, he distributed them to those who were seated; so also the fish, as much as they wanted. When they were satisfied, he told his disciples, "Gather up the fragments left over, so that nothing may be lost." So they gathered them up, and from the fragments of the five barley loaves, left by those who had eaten, they filled twelve baskets. When the people saw the sign that he had done, they began to say, "This is indeed the prophet who is to come into the world."

When Jesus realized that they were about to come and take him by force to make him king, he withdrew again to the mountain by himself.

Reflection

Nature gives us hints of how lavishly generous God is: think of a strawberry patch crowded with ripe red berries or countless brilliant wildflowers growing in a field. When Jesus miraculously multiplied the bread, twelve baskets of fragments were left over after the large crowd had eaten their fill! Jesus, the very image of God, demonstrates God's generosity with us. Likewise, an abundance of grace awaits us in the Eucharist, the Bread of Life.

Pope Francis reflects on this miracle of Jesus with us:

> Jesus speaks in silence in the mystery of the Eucharist. He reminds us every time that following him means going out of ourselves and not making our life a possession of our own, but rather a gift to him and to others.[26]

> Jesus . . . gives himself to us in the Eucharist, shares in our journey, indeed he makes himself food, the true food that sustains our life also in moments when the road becomes hard-going and obstacles slow our steps. And in the Eucharist the Lord makes us walk on his road, that of service, of sharing, of giving; and if it is shared, that little we have, that little we

are, becomes riches, for the power of God—which is the power of love—comes down into our poverty to transform it.

So let us ask ourselves . . . in adoring Christ who is really present in the Eucharist: do I let myself be transformed by him? Do I let the Lord who gives himself to me, guide me to going out ever more from my little enclosure, in order to give, to share, to love him and others?[27]

Following Jesus Way

The greatest grace of receiving Holy Communion is, of course, intimate union with Jesus himself. Jesus not only loves you just as you are, but also wants your deepest happiness, so in every Communion Jesus nourishes you, enlightens you, renews you, strengthens you, and transforms you. How are you able to see Jesus' love for you at work in your life in the past day or week? Realizing this abundance that Jesus offers you, respond with humble gratitude.

The Canticle from Saint Paul's Letter to the Ephesians sums up many of the graces we have received in Christ. Pray this Canticle now (found on page 181) in thanksgiving for the many graces we have received through the gift of the Eucharist.

Blessed James Alberione offers his insight into what it is like to be transformed by God's love:

> When [a soul perfected in love] contemplates the Host and Jesus who immolates himself on the altar, she feels like a drop lost in the ocean of love. "She sees all in One; she loves all in

One." When she contemplates nature—the sea, the mountains, flowers, fruits—she does not contemplate them for their own sake, but sees in them God the Creator, who made everything out of love. She raises herself from material things to God. God is always present and forms one thing alone with her. "It is God who offers me this delight now; it is God who permits this affliction for me."[28]

In *On the Contemplation of God*, William of Saint Thierry wrote that we cannot become who God created us to be—our truest selves—except by loving God. Just as eating bread nourishes our physical bodies, receiving the Bread of Life nourishes the life of the soul, our core identity, and our life in Christ: deepening our happiness, increasing our love, preparing us for eternal life, and strengthening us to overcome any sinfulness or weakness. How do we experience our prayer, our relationship with Jesus in the Eucharist, as life-giving?

Reflect on how you have been able to nurture others with the love and life that you have received. When has loving others felt like a struggle, perhaps even lifeless? Bring these situations to Jesus. Compare your words and actions with the words and example of Jesus and speak honestly with him about them.

Express your sorrow and trust in the Lord in your own words.

Act of Hope in Jesus' Eucharistic Presence

Jesus, sole Way of salvation, you invite us: "Learn from me." But I resemble you so little!

Lord, I am not worthy to receive you, but only say the word and I shall be healed.

Jesus, you pleased the Father; you are our Way. Draw me to yourself and give me the grace to love others as you have loved me.

Blessed James Alberione

Sharing Jesus' Life

Jesus promises: "I am the bread of life. Whoever comes to me will never be hungry, and whoever believes in me will never be thirsty" (Jn 6:35). What do you hunger for in your everyday life? What are the deeper longings of your heart, the ones you glimpse in times of quiet reflection? Take a few moments to speak to the Lord about the deepest desires of your heart, entrusting them to Jesus.

Pray the following prayer, Invocations to Jesus Master, taking time with each petition, and asking Jesus to transform your heart to become more Christ-like. Be assured that Jesus really wants to give you these gifts of grace. When you are finished, go back and pray the entire prayer again for someone you would like to pray for, substituting his or her name for "me" and "my." At the end, add your own personal invocations for that person.

Invocations to Jesus Master

Jesus Master, sanctify my mind and increase my faith.
Jesus, teaching in the Church, draw everyone to yourself.
Jesus Master, deliver me from error, empty thoughts, and spiritual blindness.
Jesus, Way between the Father and us, I offer you everything and await all from you.
Jesus, Way of sanctity, help me imitate you faithfully.
Jesus Way, may I respond wholeheartedly to the Father's call to holiness.
Jesus Life, live in me so that I may live in you.
Jesus Life, do not permit anything to separate me from you.
Jesus Life, grant that I may live eternally in the joy of your love.
Jesus Truth, may you shine in the world through me.
Jesus Way, may I faithfully mirror your example to others.
Jesus Life, may I be a channel of your grace and consolation for others.

Blessed James Alberione

Act of Love in Jesus' Eucharistic Presence

O Jesus Life, my joy and source of all good, I love you. I ask that I may love you always more, and all those you have redeemed.

You are the vine, and I am the branch; I want to remain united to you always so as to bear much fruit.

You are the source: pour out an ever-greater abundance of grace to sanctify me.

You are the head, and I am your member: communicate to me your Holy Spirit with all the Spirit's gifts.

May your kingdom come through Mary.

Console and save those dear to me. Bring those who have died into your presence. Assist all who share your mission of spreading the Good News. Bless the Church with many vocations to the priesthood and religious life. Amen.

Blessed James Alberione

As you conclude your hour of adoration, make a spiritual communion (see page 43) and ask Jesus to help you imitate his selfless love in your daily life.

Holy Hour Three

Jesus Our Way, Truth, and Life

Allowing Jesus in the Eucharist to transform your life in him.

During the Last Supper—his last night before his death on the cross—Jesus spoke from the depths of his Heart to his disciples. Take a few moments to adore Jesus who died and rose for you, who renews that sacrifice of his life daily for you, who wants so much to be part of your life that he nourishes you in Communion, who wants so much to be close to you that he remains present here in the Eucharist in silence and simplicity.

Adoring Jesus Truth

Ask the Holy Spirit, whom Jesus gave to us as our Intercessor before the Father, to flood your soul with divine light, so that you will receive the word of God fully into your heart, allowing his living word to transform your perspective, your attitudes, your feelings, your life.

Reading: John 14:1–12

"Do not let your hearts be troubled. Believe in God, believe also in me. In my Father's house there are many dwelling places. If it were not so, would I have told you that I go to prepare a place for you? And if I go and prepare a place for you, I will come again and will take you to myself, so that where I am, there you may be also. And you know the way to the place where I am going." Thomas said to him, "Lord, we do not know where you are going. How can we know the way?" Jesus said to him, "I am the way, and the truth, and the life. No one comes to the Father except through me. If you know me, you will know my Father also. From now on you do know him and have seen him."

Philip said to him, "Lord, show us the Father, and we will be satisfied." Jesus said to him, "Have I been with you all this time, Philip, and you still do not know me? Whoever has seen me has seen the Father. How can you say, 'Show us the Father'? Do you not believe that I am in the Father and the Father is in me? The words that I say to you I do not speak on my own; but the Father who dwells in me does his works. Believe me that I am in the Father and the Father is in me; but if you do not, then believe me because of the works themselves. Very truly, I tell you, the one who believes in me will also do the works that I do and, in fact, will do greater works than these, because I am going to the Father."

REFLECTION

In this powerful yet consoling passage, Jesus invites you to enter more deeply into a personal relationship with him—a relationship that can encompass any pressure, any difficulty, any joy, or trouble. Jesus wants you to experience the security of being loved faithfully, unconditionally: "Do not let your hearts be troubled."

The words, "I am the Way, and the Truth, and the Life," are not only a profound self-definition and a description of Jesus' relationship with us. They are a dazzling yet mysterious promise of loving fidelity and companionship. What might these words of Jesus mean to you?

In the paschal mystery, Jesus reveals your true value in God's eyes: the love of the Trinity poured out through Jesus for humanity, for the sake of each one of us, for your sake! Jesus' self-sacrificing love revealed in the Eucharist can become the foundation of your way of thinking, living, praying—the Truth that truly sets you free.

In his humble and self-forgetting Eucharistic presence, Jesus is your Way, your faithful Companion, and your Model for how to live in true freedom and obedience to the Father.

In transforming bread and wine into his own Body and Blood, Jesus nourishes you with his own life, literally becoming your Life and infusing comfort, strength, joy, and fruitfulness—both for you and for those whose lives you touch.

Take a few minutes to reflect on your relationship with Jesus. How is Jesus *your* Way, *your* Truth, and *your* Life? How can you enter more deeply into relationship with Jesus?

As a response to the reading, renew your faith in Jesus:

Act of Faith in Jesus' Promises

Jesus, I believe you are the Word who became flesh and lived among us, offering us grace and truth.

Jesus, I believe you are the Lamb of God who takes away our sins.

Jesus, I believe you are the Master who invites us to discipleship, growth, humility, and ever-greater love.

Jesus, I believe you are God's beloved Son, sent into the world to save us.

Jesus, I believe you are Living Water, who quenches our thirst for meaning, love, peace, and truth, offering us abundant life!

Jesus, I believe you are the Bread of Life, broken and given for the life of the world.

Jesus, I believe you are the Light of the world, who frees us from darkness and answers the deepest questions of our hearts.

Jesus, I believe you are the Good Shepherd, who laid down his life for us and keeps us safe, and who calls us to shepherd others.

Jesus, I believe you are the Resurrection, promising eternal life to all who believe in you.

Jesus, I believe you are the Master who became the servant of all.

Jesus, I believe you are the living and true Vine who promises plentiful fruit and life to all the branches remaining united to you.

Jesus, I believe you are the Way, the Truth, and the Life of the world, inviting us to enter into a relationship with the Father like your own and be transformed in you.

Following Jesus Way

Jesus invites you not only into communion with himself, but into the loving embrace of the Trinity, to share in his relationship with the Father and the Spirit. To "remain" in Jesus means to let your entire life be shaped by the absolutely faithful love of a God who pours himself out for his beloved ones.

Reflect on the ways God has poured out blessings on you: in your family, in your friendships, in your life of faith, in your vocation. How has God worked in you and through you? In your accomplishments, in your weaknesses? In the past day, week, or month? Pause to thank God in your own words.

Pondering the mystery of Jesus' Eucharistic love for you leads to the realization that you, too, are called to pour yourself out in love for God and for those whom God loves. In the reading above, Jesus reminds us that whoever believes in him will do his works of love. How is Jesus inviting you to love more deeply? How is he inviting you to do his works in your life?

Pause now to bring to Jesus those situations in your life in which you find it difficult to hear or follow his call: the challenges to holiness you face in your life. Reflect on how you handled those challenges and compare your words and actions with the words and example of Jesus.

For the times you have not loved as the Lord would have, pray:

Act of Sorrow

> Lord, you have called me "friend" and "beloved,"
> even though you know I am weak and sinful.
> I am deeply sorry for my sins,
> for having broken or weakened my communion with you,
> and with your beloved ones—each person made
>   in your image.
> I pray that your loving mercy
> will heal what I have hurt,
> strengthen what I have weakened,
> and transform me
> into a more faithful reflection of your love upon earth.

Ask Jesus to pour out his grace upon you in a very special way today, to help you to act out of the deepest core of your vocation to love—love for God and for those people God has entrusted to your care in some way.

Sharing Jesus' Life

Prayer nurtures your growth in holiness: allowing God to transform you to become more like Jesus. The Chaplet to Jesus Master, Way, Truth, and Life, was developed by Blessed James Alberione to nurture Christ's life in each of us (see page 188). Pray one or each point of the chaplet as a "launching pad" to express in your own words your desire that Christ, Way, Truth, and Life, live in you completely—mind, will, and heart.

As you conclude your hour of adoration, make a spiritual communion (see page 43) and ask Jesus to allow you to faithfully reflect his love to everyone you meet today, and especially to the first person you come across who seems "unlovable."

Holy Hour Four

Jesus, Word of Life

Inviting Jesus to bring newness of life into your particular situation.

You may wish to use this guide during Advent or Christmas to focus your prayer on the Incarnation of the Son of God.

There are seasons in life—like the busy weeks before Christmas, or during the illness of a loved one—where you may come to an hour of adoration overwhelmed by worry, fatigue, or distraction about all you have to do. That is more than okay, because God loves you just as you are and wants you to entrust yourself to him especially in the times you need him most. Take a few moments to share with the Lord whatever weighs heavy on your heart. This hour is a precious time in which you can welcome Jesus into your heart and life in a new way—this Jesus, our Savior, who wants to transform every moment of your life, no matter how difficult, into an experience of his love. He wants to embrace you, strengthen you, and lift you up into the very heart of God.

Prayer of Adoration

My Jesus, Lord,
I come to you thirsty for beauty:
so often I feel betrayed by the ugliness in the world around me,
ugliness that I sometimes help to build.
All-Beautiful One, remind me
of the inner beauty of each person created and loved by you.
I come to you thirsting for truth:
I see so much senseless suffering
and have so many questions I cannot answer.
You who are the Word of Truth,
help me to understand the real meaning of my life
so that all I do flows out of a sense of purpose,
out of your deepest call to me.
I thirst for wholeness:
our disrespect for one another tears the human family apart,
and fractures my heart a piece at a time.
You can heal the wounds that divide us,
if we let you.
Heal my heart, and the divisions in every human heart.
You who are All-Good,
I am thirsty for your goodness:

I take for granted the abundance you shower on me
   every day!
Whether I am in the dark or in the light,
let me always remember that you wish to bless me
and fill me with life.
Let me feel your hand holding mine, reminding me
that you are always with me,
encouraging me to share your own goodness
   with others.

Adoring Jesus Truth

The Prologue of the Gospel of John is a contemplative work, slowing us down to savor the amazing reality of the Incarnation: the Word of God, the Second Person of the Blessed Trinity, took on our humanity and dwells with us. We need to take our time with this passage. Try noticing which words are repeated in the reading—words that cannot contain the mystery they seek to express—and allow that repetition to become an "entryway" into pondering the mystery and giftedness of our life in Christ.

READING: JOHN 1:1–18

In the beginning was the Word, and the Word was with God, and the Word was God. He was in the beginning with God. All things came into being through him, and without him not one thing came into being. What has come into being in him was life, and the life was the light of all people. The light shines in the darkness, and the darkness did not overcome it.

There was a man sent from God, whose name was John. He came as a witness to testify to the light, so that all might believe through him. He himself was not the light, but he came to testify to the light. The true light, which enlightens everyone, was coming into the world.

He was in the world, and the world came into being through him; yet the world did not know him. He came to what was his own, and his own people did not accept him. But to all who received him, who believed in his name, he gave power to become children of God, who were born, not of blood or of the will of the flesh or of the will of man, but of God.

And the Word became flesh and lived among us, and we have seen his glory, the glory as of a father's only son, full of grace and truth. (John testified to him and cried out, "This was he of whom I said, 'He who comes after me ranks ahead of me because he was before me.'") From his fullness we have all received, grace upon grace. The law indeed was given through Moses; grace and truth came through Jesus Christ. No one has ever seen God. It is God the only Son, who is close to the Father's heart, who has made him known.

Reflection

This rich Scripture passage gives us a glimpse of "the big picture": the inner life of the Trinity, our creation in God, the Word of God entering the world and our lives. Most of the time, we need reminders of how wonderfully loving our God is, of how God creates us in love and intends us to live in love, of how God surrounds us with the fullness of grace if only we open our hearts to him.

Jesus, the Word made flesh, is your God coming to you, becoming like you, showing you how sacred your humanity is. Jesus is fully human—he ate, worked, slept, played, loved, cried, laughed, belonged to a family, and opened his Heart to the larger "family" of humanity. Jesus tangibly reveals what a truly human life is: living in communion with the Father and with each other. Jesus is also your Way to God, because he shares with you his own relationship to the Father.

Jesus wants to draw you into his vital relationship with the Father: he offers himself at every Eucharist to the Father on your behalf; he has left you the living word of the Scriptures so that he can freely speak to your heart. Jesus is the Word of Life who helps you to enter more deeply into the heart of our loving God, an encounter that can renew you and transform you every day.

Do you feel this abundance of life? Pause a few moments now to reflect on how Jesus' becoming fully human has transformed our lives.

At the Annunciation, the young Virgin Mary was completely receptive to the most unexpected coming of Jesus into her life. As you pray the Angelus, ask Mary to help you welcome Jesus with open arms, however unexpectedly he wants to come into your life. And in gratitude for the ways he has come to you, express your faith in the gift of the Incarnation, of Jesus becoming fully human, by praying the Angelus (see page 277).

Following Jesus Way

The Lord blesses you abundantly every day on many levels: the gift of life; the gift of family and friends; the ability to think, act, and love; the special relationship with God shared through your Baptism, healed in the Sacrament of Reconciliation, and nurtured in the Eucharist. Pray your personal litany of thanksgiving by calling to mind all the gifts for which you wish to thank God.

In thanksgiving, pray the Canticle from Isaiah (see page 175), in which God is inviting Israel to partake of and celebrate the abundance that God offers to us.

You have just reflected on the abundance that Jesus, the Word of Life, brings to all of us by sharing our humanity. But like most of us, you probably have areas in your life that remain in shadow, that seem untouched by the light and joy that Jesus brings. In the Letter to the Romans, Saint Paul says, "We know that all things work together for good for those who love God, who are called according to his purpose" (Rom 8:28).

Pause now to bring to Jesus one aspect of yourself or of your life that seems to drain you or drag you down. Ask Jesus to begin to transform this place of struggle, death, uncertainty, or darkness into something life-giving.

Make an act of sorrow for your sinfulness, for the times when you have allowed a tendency to death, not life, reign in you:

Act of Sorrow

Loving Savior, you suffered, died, and rose to save us. Fill us with joy and newness of life. Forgive us for the times that we have given in to the darkness of sin: for our weakness in doing good, for doubting your love and your promises, for selfishly holding onto your free gifts to us, for being so self-absorbed that we don't even notice the needs of those around us. Let us again "be baptized into your death" so that we may also live your risen life; make us signs of joy and newness of life for those around us. Amen.

In the book of the prophet Isaiah, God promises: "I will give you the treasures of darkness" (Is 45:3). Entrust your own situation of darkness to the Lord, expressing your trust that God will fulfill this promise of bringing hope out of darkness, fulfillment after a time of waiting, newness of life out of death.

Sharing Jesus' Life

"To Jesus through Mary" has been the motto of many saints. We turn to Mary, Jesus' Mother and most faithful disciple, to ask her intercession for the intentions and desires we have brought to this holy hour. As you pray the Joyful Mysteries of the Rosary (see page 258), you may wish to focus on the ways that Mary welcomed Jesus and then shared him with others throughout her life.

If you have time, pray again the Prologue of the Gospel of John, this time as a hymn of praise to Jesus, the Word of Life, who allows you to share in his sonship as God's beloved.

As you conclude your hour of adoration, make a spiritual communion (see page 43) and ask Jesus for the gift to recognize the newness of life he brings you each day, and how to foster new life in others, whether by an encouraging word, a sharing of material goods, or by a witness of your joy in Christ.

Holy Hour Five

With Jesus Crucified

Contemplating the mystery of the crucified Jesus.

This guide may be used particularly during Lent, or any time you wish to focus your prayer on Jesus' sacrificial offering to the Father on our behalf.

Approaching the passion and death of Jesus can be difficult. Even the Gospel accounts are terse, stripped of emotion—perhaps because when expressing such a great mystery of love, words seem inadequate. Yet, this great mystery of God's great love for you and all of humanity will bear endless fruit in your life if you allow it. In this precious time with Jesus, ask for the grace to live the mystery of the Cross in your daily life: both in your joys and in your sufferings.

Adoring Jesus Truth

Meditating on the suffering, passion, and death of Jesus on the cross can be uncomfortable, leading us to feel guilty, to think more about our own suffering or where we have felt disconnected from God's saving love.

But when contemplated in the light of faith, the passion and death of Christ can become a great source of strength and consolation, especially in times of darkness and suffering.

> When we look at the crucifix, our primary feeling should not be sadness but rather adoration, contemplation, and gratitude for the salvation that was accomplished in the mystery of life offered on the wood of the cross. On this wood, Christ reigns and draws everyone to himself, because the Cross is the pathway to Resurrection.[29]

READING: JOHN 19:16–30

> Then he [Pilate] handed him over to them to be crucified.
>
> So they took Jesus; and carrying the cross by himself, he went out to what is called The Place of the Skull, which in Hebrew is called Golgotha. There they crucified him, and with him two others, one on either side, with Jesus between them. Pilate also had an inscription written and put on the cross. It read, "Jesus of Nazareth, the King of the Jews." Many of the Jews read this inscription, because the place where Jesus was crucified was near the city; and it was written in Hebrew, in Latin, and in Greek. Then the chief priests of the Jews said to Pilate, "Do not write, 'The King of the Jews,' but, 'This man said, I am King of the Jews.'" Pilate answered, "What I have written I have written." When the soldiers had crucified Jesus, they took his clothes and divided them into four parts, one for each soldier. They also took his tunic; now the tunic was seamless, woven in one piece from the top. So they said to

one another, "Let us not tear it, but cast lots for it to see who will get it." This was to fulfill what the scripture says,

"They divided my clothes among themselves,
and for my clothing they cast lots."

And that is what the soldiers did.

Meanwhile, standing near the cross of Jesus were his mother, and his mother's sister, Mary the wife of Clopas, and Mary Magdalene. When Jesus saw his mother and the disciple whom he loved standing beside her, he said to his mother, "Woman, here is your son." Then he said to the disciple, "Here is your mother." And from that hour the disciple took her into his own home.

After this, when Jesus knew that all was now finished, he said (in order to fulfill the scripture), "I am thirsty." A jar full of sour wine was standing there. So they put a sponge full of the wine on a branch of hyssop and held it to his mouth. When Jesus had received the wine, he said, "It is finished." Then he bowed his head and gave up his spirit.

REFLECTION

What impressed you in this reading? What does it stir up in you? Do you believe that Jesus' death 2,000 years ago was for you, individually? What do you wish you could have told Jesus that first Good Friday?

One way to meditate on Christ's passion and death is to reread the Gospel passage and imagine yourself standing beneath the Cross, at the side of John and Mary, his Mother.

You may wish to speak to him, but if no words come, just stay with him in his suffering.

At every Mass, Jesus renews his supreme sacrifice of love for us: the Mass is the re-presentation of Jesus' great act of love and self-offering to the Father on our behalf. Pray the hymn, "Godhead Here in Hiding," as an act of faith in Christ's saving love for you, perhaps also asking for the grace to allow Jesus to transform you (see page 288).

Following Jesus Way

Saint John Paul II has written powerfully about Jesus' saving love, which we are privileged to witness every time we go to Mass:

> When we are shaken by the sight of evil spreading in the universe . . . we should not forget that such unleashing of the forces of sin is overcome by the saving power of Christ. Whenever the words of consecration are uttered in the Mass and the Body and Blood of Christ become present in the act of the sacrifice, the triumph of love over hatred, of holiness over sin, is also present. Every Eucharistic Celebration is stronger than all the evil in the universe; it means real, concrete accomplishment of the Redemption.[30]

The night before he died, Jesus told his disciples, "No one has greater love than this, to lay down one's life for one's friends" (John 15:13). How have you prayed with Jesus dying for love of you? How have you thanked him for this incredible act of love?

As an act of thanksgiving for the great gift of Jesus' renewing the sacrifice of his love for you at every Mass, pray Cardinal John Carberry's Act of Adoration (see page 196).

Knowing that you have been loved so deeply by Jesus, how do you want to love Jesus in return? A classic definition of love is willing the good of the other. The most concrete way to show your love for Jesus is to fulfill the new commandment that Jesus gave right before his death: "Love one another as I have loved you" (Jn. 15:12). Christ laid down his life for us. How is he calling you to "lay down" your life (your preferences, your time, your possessions) for others today? Is there someone in your life whom you struggle with loving?

Pause to reflect on challenges you face in living Jesus' commandment to love others as he has loved us, comparing your choices with his words and example. What holds you back from loving selflessly?

Express your sorrow for the times you have failed to love, by praying an Act of Contrition (see pages 217ff.) and these invocations to the Heart of Jesus:

Heart of Jesus, Son of the eternal Father, *have mercy on us.*
Heart of Jesus, broken for our sins, *have mercy on us.*
Heart of Jesus, our peace and reconciliation, *have mercy on us.*

Ask our loving Eucharistic Master to fill you with his love, his life, his grace, so that you can share them with others by praying the beautiful Anima Christi (see pages 50/51).

Sharing Jesus' Life

To deepen your consideration of how much Jesus has loved you, you can pray the Stations of the Cross (see pages 229ff.). Or you may wish to choose one scene from Jesus' passion that has always stood out for you and imagine yourself there; simply be there with Jesus and speak to him from your heart.

As you conclude your hour of adoration, make a spiritual communion (see page 43) and ask Jesus for the gift of making a special act of love today towards someone you have a hard time loving or getting along with—an act that imitates Jesus' sacrificial love for you.

Holy Hour Six

"I Am with You"

Sharing a particular sorrow or difficulty with the Lord.

In times of difficulty or sorrow, it can be hard to pray. In this hour, you are invited to open your heart to God and ask God to be with you in all that you are experiencing. Spend a few moments in silent adoration. Ask for the light of the Holy Spirit so that you may feel God's presence and receive comfort.

If during this prayer time you do not feel the presence of the Lord with you, don't be disturbed. Feeling that God is far away is a common experience, especially in times of suffering. Psalm 34 reminds us that God is near to the brokenhearted. If no words come to you during this time of prayer, just try to remember that you are in God's loving presence. That in itself is a powerful prayer of faith. Later in this hour, you will be invited to offer your sufferings with and to Jesus, in reparation for sins against the Holy Eucharist.

Adoring Jesus Truth

In this reading, Jesus raises Lazarus from the dead. But first, he weeps with Martha and Mary over the loss of their brother. How is God with you in this time of difficulty? Is God weeping with you? Drying your tears? Embracing you?

READING: JOHN 11:1–3, 17–36, 38–44

Now a certain man was ill, Lazarus of Bethany, the village of Mary and her sister Martha. Mary was the one who anointed the Lord with perfume and wiped his feet with her hair; her brother Lazarus was ill. So the sisters sent a message to Jesus, "Lord, he whom you love is ill."

... When Jesus arrived, he found that Lazarus had already been in the tomb for four days. Now Bethany was near Jerusalem, some two miles away, and many of the Jews had come to Martha and Mary to console them about their brother. When Martha heard that Jesus was coming, she went and met him, while Mary stayed at home. Martha said to Jesus, "Lord, if you had been here, my brother would not have died. But even now I know that God will give you whatever you ask of him." Jesus said to her, "Your brother will rise again." Martha said to him, "I know that he will rise again in the resurrection on the last day." Jesus said to her, "I am the resurrection and the life. Those who believe in me, even though they die, will live, and everyone who lives and believes in me will never die. Do you believe this?" She said to him, "Yes, Lord, I believe that you are the Messiah, the Son of God, the one coming into the world."

When she had said this, she went back and called her sister Mary, and told her privately, "The Teacher is here and is calling for you." And when she heard it, she got up quickly and went to him. Now Jesus had not yet come to the village, but was still at the place where Martha had met him. The Jews who were with her in the house, consoling her, saw Mary get up quickly and go out. They followed her because they thought that she was going to the tomb to weep there. When Mary came where Jesus was and saw him, she knelt at his feet and said to him, "Lord, if you had been here, my brother would not have died." When Jesus saw her weeping, and the Jews who came with her also weeping, he was greatly disturbed in spirit and deeply moved. He said, "Where have you laid him?" They said to him, "Lord, come and see." Jesus began to weep. So the Jews said, "See how he loved him!"

... Then Jesus, again greatly disturbed, came to the tomb. It was a cave, and a stone was lying against it. Jesus said, "Take away the stone." Martha, the sister of the dead man, said to him, "Lord, already there is a stench because he has been dead four days." Jesus said to her, "Did I not tell you that if you believed, you would see the glory of God?" So they took away the stone. And Jesus looked upward and said, "Father, I thank you for having heard me. I knew that you always hear me, but I have said this for the sake of the crowd standing here, so that they may believe that you sent me." When he had said this, he cried with a loud voice, "Lazarus, come out!" The dead man came out, his hands and feet bound with strips of cloth, and his face wrapped in a cloth. Jesus said to them, "Unbind him, and let him go."

Reflection

As Jesus arrives to console Martha and Mary, and to raise their brother Lazarus from the dead, Martha runs to her sister Mary and tells her, "The Master is here and wants to see you." What powerful words these must have been to the grieving Mary. These words are addressed to you, too. Jesus Master wants to meet you here, where you are. He wants you to sit with him and share your sorrows, your suffering, your fears, and your pain.

After some quiet reflection, pray the following act of faith as a response to the reading.

An Act of Faith in the Lord's Faithful Presence

> Lord, I believe you are here with me right now, loving me.
> But it's dark and I cannot see your radiance.
> It's quiet and I cannot hear the tender whisper of your voice.
> My heart is so broken and afraid
> that I cannot feel the warmth of your gentle presence.
> I can only pray: Be with me, Lord.
> I want to see your face.
> I want to know that you are with me.
> I want to be cradled in your arms.
> I want to feel your strength, your peace.
> Even if I can't feel you, hold me tight.
> Even if I can't see you, stay right beside me.

Even in the darkest hour, be with me, Lord.

You are the Divine Master: help me to discover your presence in every situation.

You walked the way of suffering during your earthly life: now walk with me.

You are the Resurrection and the Life, overcoming sin and death: fill me with your grace and love.

I cling to your promise: "Do not be afraid, for I am with you always, until the very end of time." I entrust myself completely to your merciful love.

Following Jesus Way

The night before Jesus died, he went to pray in the Garden of Gethsemane, and he asked his three disciples, Peter, James, and John, to watch and pray with him. They fell asleep, and Jesus was left all alone in the night. (See Lk 22:39–46.) Ask Jesus now to "watch and pray" with you as you face this difficult time. Ask him to be with you and to help you discover his presence in your suffering. Listen to Jesus' voice, calling you to grow or respond in this situation.

As you compare your life with Jesus' words and example, choose to focus not on your weakness, but on God's presence and love for you.

Renew your trust in the Lord by holding in your mind or repeating aloud a phrase that reminds you that God is with you, such as "God is near to the brokenhearted."

Sharing Jesus' Life

At difficult times, one of the best ways to pray is to pour out your heart to the Lord, sharing with God your deepest feelings—anger, discouragement, fears, hopes, and desires.

The psalms are wonderful, honest prayers of the heart. When he was dying on the cross, Jesus quoted one of the psalms, Psalm 31. After you have talked heart-to-heart with the Lord, pray this psalm (see page 162), making it your heart's cry to the God who loves you.

As you ask God to be your refuge and strength, can you unite your moment of suffering with Jesus' sufferings on the cross? Theologians and mystics tell us that Jesus' greatest sufferings were not physical—as tortuous as they were—but were sufferings caused by the sins of those who reject him. Perhaps you can "watch and pray" with Jesus and offer this moment of suffering in reparation to Jesus for the sins of neglect, disrespect, and sacrilege towards his most vulnerable presence in the Blessed Sacrament. You may wish to pray with the Litany to the Precious Blood (see page 222), or one of the acts of reparation (found on pages 217–235).

As you conclude your hour of adoration, carry these words of comfort and trust from Saint Paul's Letter to the Romans with you:

> If God is for us, who is against us? He who did not withhold his own Son, but gave him up for all of us, will he not with him also give us everything else? Who will bring any charge

against God's elect? It is God who justifies. Who is to condemn? It is Christ Jesus, who died, yes, who was raised, who is at the right hand of God, who indeed intercedes for us. Who will separate us from the love of Christ? Will hardship, or distress, or persecution, or famine, or nakedness, or peril, or sword?

[Add your own fears.]

As it is written,
"For your sake we are being killed all day long;
we are accounted as sheep to be slaughtered."

No, in all these things we are more than conquerors through him who loved us. For I am convinced that neither death, nor life, nor angels, nor rulers, nor things present, nor things to come, nor powers, nor height, nor depth, nor anything else in all creation, will be able to separate us from the love of God in Christ Jesus our Lord (Rom 8:31–39).

Holy Hour Seven

Praising God with Christ, Our Risen Savior

Offering praise and thanksgiving to God in Christ, our Risen Savior.

Begin this hour of adoration by praying or singing a favorite hymn that praises God's goodness. If this hour is prayed in a group, music or singing should be used throughout this hour as much as possible to express a joyful spirit of praise.

The more you recognize God's presence and work in your life, the easier it is to take to heart the important truth that Saint Paul reminds us about in his First Letter to the Corinthians, "What do you have that you did not receive?" (1 Cor 4:7) Everything you have is a gratuitous gift from God, who created you out of love and owes you nothing. It is only fitting that gratitude and praise be an important part of your prayer.

Thanksgiving doesn't just glorify God: it can also uplift you, becoming a source of great joy and peace for you by helping you focus on God's goodness and love. In this hour of adoration, celebrate the many blessings God has bestowed on you. The very word "Eucharist" means thanksgiving: Jesus's saving sacrifice of his life and Resurrection is first of all an act of adoration and love offered to the Father, for love of us. When you pray in thanksgiving at Mass and in the presence of the Holy Eucharist, you unite your praise of God with that perfect praise that Jesus offers to the Father.

Adoring Jesus Truth

The Pauline Letters exhort believers dozens of times to give thanks, pointing out many reasons for joy and gratitude. This small selection of readings show how thanksgiving is an integral part of one's relationship with Christ and, through Christ, with the Father.

Reading: 1 Thessalonians 5:16–24

Rejoice always, pray without ceasing, give thanks in all circumstances; for this is the will of God in Christ Jesus for you. Do not quench the Spirit. Do not despise the words of prophets, but test everything; hold fast to what is good; abstain from every form of evil.

May the God of peace himself sanctify you entirely; and may your spirit and soul and body be kept sound and blameless at the coming of our Lord Jesus Christ. The one who calls you is faithful, and he will do this.

Reading: Philippians 4:4–7

Rejoice in the Lord always; again I will say, Rejoice. Let your gentleness be known to everyone. The Lord is near. Do not worry about anything, but in everything by prayer and supplication with thanksgiving let your requests be made known to God. And the peace of God, which surpasses all understanding, will guard your hearts and your minds in Christ Jesus.

Reading: Ephesians 2:4–10

God, who is rich in mercy, out of the great love with which he loved us even when we were dead through our trespasses, made us alive together with Christ—by grace you have been saved—and raised us up with him and seated us with him in the heavenly places in Christ Jesus, so that in the ages to come he might show the immeasurable riches of his grace in kindness toward us in Christ Jesus. For by grace you have been saved through faith, and this is not your own doing; it is the gift of God—not the result of works, so that no one may boast. For we are what he has made us, created in Christ Jesus for good works, which God prepared beforehand to be our way of life.

Reflection

These readings encourage reflection on how God has proven his faithfulness, especially in Christ Jesus. Christ reveals his love for you in innumerable ways: creating you, redeeming you from the power of sin, blessing you, choosing you out of love to be holy, embracing you as brother or sister, promising you eternal life.... What are some of the "immeasurable riches" that you have received? Is there a phrase in one of these readings that helps you to realize in a fresh way God's overwhelming love for you? As you consider the many graces you have received, what grace has helped you the most spiritually? In your thanksgiving include your gratitude for the gift of the Holy Eucharist with the prayer the Divine Praises (on page 64), followed by Psalm 116 (on page 167).

Following Jesus Way

God has worked in your life in wondrous ways. Yet it can often be easy to take for granted the gifts God gives so freely, lovingly, and tenderly. Each gift, each moment of life, is too precious to let slip by.

Look at your hands for a few moments. Hold them open, palms up, on your lap or stretched out in front of you. Your hands receive so many things every day. Think of the things your hands have grasped today or in the past week: the support of a railing on the stairs, a friendly handshake, a sandwich, a book, Holy Communion.... Each time you open your hands, you receive a gift. Some of these gifts are welcomed fully. Others are barely noticed. Unnoticed gifts are often never unwrapped, seen for what they are, or appreciated.

Take a few moments now to pray with your hands. Let your open hands symbolize a welcoming heart ready to receive the graces God wants to give: much-needed graces that are overlooked; graces that could amaze you; graces that are waiting for you if you are open to receiving them.

God has given so much to each of us. Aware of the many graces you have received, pause to reflect on the ways you have responded to the invitations hidden within each grace. How generous God has been to you! How generously have you shared these gifts, especially the ones that mean the most to you? What challenges do you face in sharing your time and your love with others?

Jesus wants to give you the fullness of life and wants you to share that life with others. Acknowledge God's goodness to you—for all the graces you have received, but especially for his free forgiveness—in the words of this simple but profound prayer:

My Lord, I am entirely the work of your omnipotent love.

I adore you, my God, one in nature and triune in Persons.

I thank you, because you have made me for the happiness that lies in you and for your eternal glory. Save me with your omnipotence, your love, and your mercy!

Blessed James Alberione

Sharing Jesus' Life

The Creed of the Called is drawn from the Pauline letters and focuses on the relationship between the disciple and the Father—how we have received everything from God and how God calls us to share with others what we have received, trusting that God will work in and through our lives.

Creed of the Called

We believe that God chose us in him before the world began, to be holy and blameless in his sight.

We believe that those whom he foreknew he predestined to share the image of his Son.

We believe that God who set us apart before we were born and called us by his favor chose to reveal his Son to us, that we might spread among all people the good tidings concerning him.

We believe that God has saved us and has called us to a holy life, not because of any merit of ours but according to his own design—the grace held out to us in Christ Jesus before the world began.

We believe that Christ Jesus has judged us faithful and worthy by calling us to his service.

We believe that we are apostles by vocation, servants of Christ Jesus, set apart to announce the Gospel of God.

Considering our vocation, we believe that God chose the weak of this world to shame the strong, so that our faith would not rest on human wisdom but on the power of God.

We believe that to each one God has given the manifestation of the Spirit for the common good.

We believe that we must live a life worthy of the calling we have received: with perfect humility, meekness, and patience, seeking to grow in all things toward him.

We believe that all things work together for the good of those who love God, who have been called according to his decree.

We believe in him whose power now at work in us can do immeasurably more than we ask or imagine.

We believe that he who has begun the good work in us will carry it through to completion, right up to the day of Christ Jesus, because he who calls us is faithful.

If you have time, you may wish to add a personal litany of thanksgiving in your own words, listing your many reasons for joy followed by a response of gratitude or praise, such as, "I praise you, Lord."

As you conclude your adoration, choose one way that you can practice this spirit of gratitude in your daily life.

Holy Hour Eight

Called by Jesus the Good Shepherd

*Responding in trust and love to Jesus the Good Shepherd,
who leads you, guides you, and calls you to "shepherd" one another.*

You may come to this hour of adoration distracted or tired or worried and that's okay, because God loves you just as you are and wants you to entrust yourself to him—all that you are, feel, do—all that concerns you. Take a few moments to speak to the Lord about what weighs heavy on your heart. This hour is a precious time in which you can focus your attention on Jesus' shepherding love for you, so that you can be nurtured, strengthened, called, and lifted up into the very heart of God.

Prayer of Presence

> We adore you, Jesus,
> eternal Shepherd of the human race.
> You are present in the Eucharist
> to dwell continually in the midst of your people.
> You nourish us, you guard us,

you guide us to the heavenly fold.
We do not live on bread alone,
but on your word of truth and love.
We listen to your voice
and follow it with love.
Give us the grace to listen to and love your word,
that it may bear fruit in our hearts.
Speak, Lord, your servant is listening.

Blessed James Alberione

Adoring Jesus Truth

The Good Shepherd is a comforting image, representing God's fidelity and nurturing love for us and for others. Jesus is always with us on life's journey.

READING JOHN 10:11–18

"I am the good shepherd. The good shepherd lays down his life for the sheep. The hired hand, who is not the shepherd and does not own the sheep, sees the wolf coming and leaves the sheep and runs away—and the wolf snatches them and scatters them. The hired hand runs away because a hired hand does not care for the sheep. I am the good shepherd. I know my own and my own know me, just as the Father knows me and I know the Father. And I lay down my life for the sheep. I have other sheep that do not belong to this fold. I must bring them also, and they will listen to my voice. So there will be one flock, one shepherd. For this reason the Father loves me, because I lay down my life in order to take it up again. No one takes it from me, but I lay it down of my own accord. I have power to lay it down, and I have power to take it up again. I have received this command from my Father."

John 10 highlights many details about the relationship between a good shepherd and his sheep: The shepherd calls each sheep by name, personally leading them; the sheep recognize the shepherd's voice; the shepherd would willingly give his life to save his sheep. It's a warm, intimate picture of the trusting relationship between shepherd and sheep.

Jesus calls himself the Good Shepherd who leads and accompanies you wherever you go. Jesus leads you to the Father, wanting to bring you to fullness of life. What is the next step Jesus is asking you to take? Do you trust that the Lord will be with you? What are the obstacles that prevent you from stepping forward with Jesus?

As an act of faith, pray Psalm 100, which celebrates our relationship with God as our Shepherd (see page 167).

Following Jesus Way

In what ways have you felt shepherded by God? As you reflect on the ways that God has taken care of you, pray with gratitude Psalm 23 (see page 161).

Read the following Parable of the Lost Sheep, picturing yourself as the lamb being picked up with joy by the Shepherd:

> So he told them this parable: "Which one of you, having a hundred sheep and losing one of them, does not leave the ninety-nine in the wilderness and go after the one that is lost until he finds it? When he has found it, he lays it on his shoulders and rejoices. And when he comes home, he calls together his friends and neighbors, saying to them, 'Rejoice with me, for I have found my sheep that was lost.' Just so, I tell you, there will be more joy in heaven over one sinner who repents than over ninety-nine righteous people who need no repentance" (Lk 15:3–7).

In what area(s) of your life do you feel lost or hurt? What do you feel unable to cope with? Is there a situation in which you find it difficult to trust God? Our Good Shepherd desires to embrace and heal you, even in your most hidden or wounded places. Can you bring these areas of your life to Christ?

Perhaps the Holy Spirit has invited you to be a "good shepherd" to someone else. How have you responded to these invitations? Can you "hear" the Holy Spirit inviting you now in this way?

Express your sorrow and trust in the Lord with this prayer:

To Jesus, the Good Shepherd

> We thank you, Jesus Good Shepherd,
> for having come down from heaven

to seek out humankind
and bring us back to the way of salvation.
You are the Good Shepherd
who gathers and cares
for the scattered sheep.
The shepherd leads
and the sheep follow
because they recognize the shepherd's voice.
You have given your commandments,
your counsels, your examples.
Whoever heeds them is nourished
with a bread that does not perish:
"My food is to do the will of the heavenly Father."
Have mercy on us when we try to nourish ourselves
on falsehood or empty pleasures.
Recall us to your way.
Sustain us when we waver, strengthen us when
    we are weak.
May everyone follow you,
Shepherd and Guardian of our souls.
You alone are the Way,
you alone have words of eternal life.
We will follow you wherever you go.

Blessed James Alberione

Sharing Jesus' Life

Servant of God Dorothy Day wrote,

We cannot love God unless we love each other, and to love we must know each other. We know him in the breaking of bread, and we know each other in the breaking of bread, and we are not alone anymore. Heaven is a banquet and life is a banquet, too, even with a crust, where there is companionship.

We have all known the long loneliness and we have learned that the only solution is love and that love comes with community.[31]

The gift that Jesus makes of himself to you in the Eucharist is meant for you to share with others. Reflecting on the parable of the Lost Sheep, which you just prayed with, call to mind a situation that needs Jesus' light and grace. Perhaps someone you know is going through a really hard time, or perhaps a recent news story that is happening locally or across the globe has impressed you. Ask Jesus to bring an abundance of life to the people involved. In praying for them open your heart to the needs of the world and share Jesus' life with them in prayer.

Who else do you want to pray for, that they receive an abundance of Jesus' life? You may wish to pray the Rosary or the Divine Mercy Chaplet for these intentions.

As you conclude your prayer for the needs of your loved ones and of the world, pray to the Holy Spirit to help you to be a "good shepherd" to others you meet in the coming week.

Invocations to the Holy Spirit

Spirit of Faith, help us overcome the difficulties and trials of life.

Spirit of Truth, give us delight in every word that comes from the mouth of God.

Spirit of Light, illumine the darkness.

Spirit of Fidelity, make us faithful witnesses of your love.

Spirit of Piety, pray in us with a longing that cannot be expressed in words.

Spirit of Life, live in us with your life of grace and love.

Spirit of Newness, reawaken in us daily a new heart and a new spirit.

Spirit of Fruitfulness, produce in us living waters, flowing out to all who thirst.

Spirit of Adoption, renew in us the awareness that we are all children of God.

Spirit of Holiness, fashion and protect in us the image of the Son, so that we may become as the Father has predestined us.

Spirit of Power, conquer through strength and mildness every obstacle to grace, both within and without.

Spirit of Glory, draw everyone together, that we may be one with you, with the Father and the Son, united forever in the kingdom of eternal love.

Mary Leonora Wilson, FSP

Concluding Prayer

May you be blessed, O Jesus, who died on the cross for us! You, the innocent One, died to restore life to the guilty sheep: "I have come that they may have life and have it more abundantly." You nourish us with your life in Baptism, in Confirmation, in Penance, and in the Eucharist. May you live in every person with your Spirit! Bring back to your fold all those who are separated from you, for they are like branches cut off from the vine. We pray to you for the Church, which you acquired with the price of your Blood. May it spread throughout the world and be for everyone a sign of unity and salvation. We want to love you with all our mind, all our strength, and all our heart. For your love, I want to spend myself totally for your people.

Blessed James Alberione

As you conclude your time of adoration, make a spiritual communion (see page 43). In the day ahead, pay attention to those around you, noticing who may be struggling, feel lost, or need some assistance, and offer what help you can.

Holy Hour Nine

Eucharistic Disciples

Seeking to imitate the humility and service of Jesus in the Holy Eucharist.

Christ's way of life was one of love—love for the Father and for each person made in God's image. Jesus Master invites you to follow his example of loving service. Spend a few moments in silent adoration of the Master who loves you so much.

Adoring Jesus Truth

Ask the Holy Spirit to set your heart on fire with love, so that its light may help you see in a new way and its heat may melt away your resistance to Jesus' invitation to serve.

Reading John 13:1–15

Now before the festival of the Passover, Jesus knew that his hour had come to depart from this world and go to the Father. Having loved his own who were in the world, he loved them to the end. The devil had already put it into the heart of Judas son of Simon Iscariot to betray him. And during supper Jesus, knowing that the Father had given all things into his hands, and that he had come from God and was going to God, got up from the table, took off his outer robe, and tied a towel around himself. Then he poured water into a basin and began to wash the disciples' feet and to wipe them with the towel that was tied around him. He came to Simon Peter, who said to him, "Lord, are you going to wash my feet?" Jesus answered, "You do not know now what I am doing, but later you will understand." Peter said to him, "You will never wash my feet." Jesus answered, "Unless I wash you, you have no share with me." Simon Peter said to him, "Lord, not my feet only but also my hands and my head!" Jesus said to him, "One who has bathed does not need to wash, except for the feet, but is entirely clean. And you are clean, though not all of you." For he knew who was to betray him; for this reason he said, "Not all of you are clean."

After he had washed their feet, had put on his robe, and had returned to the table, he said to them, "Do you know what I have done to you? You call me Teacher and Lord—and you are right, for that is what I am. So if I, your Lord and Teacher, have washed your feet, you also ought to wash one another's feet. For I have set you an example, that you also should do as I have done to you."

Reflection

Many artists have depicted Jesus washing the feet of Jesus. One beautiful painting by Sieger Köder, "The Washing of Feet," shows Jesus bent over, almost crouched to the floor, with his face hidden. Peter is leaning over Jesus, familiarly placing one hand on Jesus' shoulder. But Peter's other hand is thrust out as if to push Jesus away in dismay. These gestures reflect Peter's words to Jesus. Perhaps Peter felt unworthy of Jesus' loving gesture. Or perhaps Peter felt the same unworthiness that we sometimes feel when we realize we are loved unconditionally. What would you have felt or done in Peter's place? Jesus loves you with the same intensity and proved this love, not by washing your feet, but by dying and rising for love of you. How have you received his love?

In coming to us in Holy Communion, Jesus selflessly shares his own life with us—for our own sakes, but also so that we can share his life, his love, with others. Oblate of Mary Immaculate and noted spiritual writer Ronald Rolheiser wrote in one of his columns,

> We should be on our knees washing each others' feet because that is precisely what Jesus did at the first Eucharist, teaching us that the Eucharist is not a private act of devotion, meant to square our debts with God, but a call *to* and a grace *for* service. The Eucharist sends us out into the world ready to give expression to Christ's hospitality, humility, and self-effacement.
>
> Where do we get such a notion? It lies at very the heart of the Eucharist itself. Jesus tells us this when he gives us the Eucharist, with the words: "Receive, give thanks, break, and share." The Eucharist invites us to receive nourishment from God, to be filled with gratitude, and, on the basis of that, to break open our lives and serve the poor in hospitality, humility, and self-donation.[32]

To Jesus' Gentle Heart

Jesus, Divine Master, we thank and praise your most gentle Heart, which led you to give your life for us. Your Blood, your wounds, the scourges, the thorns, the Cross, your bowed head—all tell our hearts: "No one loves more than he who gives his life for the loved one." The Shepherd died to give life to the sheep. We too want to spend our lives for you. Grant that always, everywhere, and in all things we may seek to know your will in our lives. Inflame our hearts with a deep love for you and for others.

Blessed James Alberione

Following Jesus Way

Take a few moments to thank Jesus for the many ways he has shown his love for you throughout your life. Make Saint Paul's great hymn to love your thanksgiving:

> Love is patient; love is kind; love is not envious or boastful or arrogant or rude. It does not insist on its own way; it is not irritable or resentful; it does not rejoice in wrongdoing, but rejoices in the truth. It bears all things, believes all things, hopes all things, endures all things.
>
> Love never ends. (1 Cor 13:4–8)

Jesus said, "I have set you an example, that you also should do as I have done to you" (Jn 13:15). Jesus' example of loving service challenges all of us to look into our own lives and evaluate our love in light of his. We are Jesus' hands and feet to serve those in need in our own day. Jesus *wants* to act through us.

The painting of Sieger Köder has a detail with profound implications. Although Jesus' face cannot be seen directly, his reflection can be glimpsed in the water in the basin at Peter's feet. Perhaps Köder was trying to share an insight: it is in serving others that we discover the face of Christ.

How do you feel Jesus calling you to serve others in your everyday life? Compare how you respond to that call with the words and example of Jesus.

Express your sorrow to the Lord with the following litany:

For the times I have been impatient, ℟. *Lord, have mercy!*

For the times I have been unkind, ℟.

For the times I have acted jealously, ℟.

For my prideful boasting, ℟.

For having acted arrogantly, ℟.

For having acted dishonestly, ℟.

For those times when I have acted selfishly, ℟.

For responding irritably to others, ℟.

For my brooding over past wrongs, ℟.

For the times I rejoiced not in truth, but at injustice, ℟.

For the times when I gave up on others, ℟.

For my lack of faith and hope, ℟.

For setting limits to my love, ℟.

Despite your weaknesses and fears, Jesus invites you, "Come, follow me!" Ask Jesus to show you how he is calling you to serve him more faithfully today, and ask for the grace of self-emptying love:

Prayer to Imitate Jesus, Divine Servant

Christ Jesus, transform my mind and heart so that I can more faithfully serve you. Give me your own perspective: respect for my dignity as created in the image of God, without pretending that I am equal to God or above others. Empty me of self-importance and grant me humility—the ability to fully accept the truth about my place in the world. Form me into your faithful and loving servant. Grant me the ability to recognize when to put others' needs ahead of my own. Bless me with compassion, patience, kindness, and perseverance in serving others. May I be attentive and responsive to God's call to serve, even when it is not easy. When I feel the weight of others' burdens, help me to recognize that you are with me and help me to carry the load. May my love for others be a reflection of your love. I worship you as my Lord and Master, the One who came not to be served, but to serve. Help me to be faithful to your word: "Love one another as I have loved you."

Sharing Jesus' Life

Jesus' lasting command is to love one another as he has loved us. Reach out in prayer now to others and bring before the Eucharistic Jesus the intentions of the world: the people who struggle with the darkness of pain, violence, war, abuse, disease, selfishness.

Now ask Jesus to transform you into a servant who is attentive to the needs of others and reaches out in love.

Litany of Service

(Based on Isaiah 42, 49, 50 and 52)

Lord, I believe that I am your chosen servant whom you uphold. *Send your spirit upon me.*

Lord, I believe that you have taken me by the hand and formed me. *Make me a light for those in darkness.*

Lord, I believe you called me before I was born and named me. *Make me your faithful servant through whom you will be glorified.*

Lord, sometimes I think I have worked in vain and that I have spent my strength for nothing. *Help me remember that you are my strength, and my reward is in you.*

Lord, each morning you open my ears that I may hear and speak your words: comfort to the weary, encouragement to those who are oppressed. *The Lord God helps me.*

Lord, I offer whatever I suffer as a way to share in the hardships suffered by your people. *Give me the peace of surrender to your will and the courage to oppose oppression.*

(Add your own petitions to become a more faithful servant. Pray about one way in which you can go beyond the ordinary scope of your daily life to reach out to those who are suffering.)

Concluding Prayer

Lord, I am an earthenware vessel in which you have placed a treasure. Help me to reveal your extraordinary power. When I feel afflicted, free me from constraints. When I am perplexed, lead me beyond despair. When I feel persecuted, do not forsake me. When I am struck down, renew your life in me. As I carry within myself the death of Jesus, may the life of Jesus, too, be revealed in me. Help me to realize that death at work in me means life to those for whom I offer myself. Do not let me lose heart, but grant me abundant grace, so that my thanksgiving may overflow to the glory of God (based on 2 Cor 4).

As you conclude your adoration, make a spiritual communion (see page 43). Choose a particular person or group of people who are suffering to carry in your heart and prayers this week.

Holy Hour Ten

Mary, Woman of the Eucharist

*Allowing Mary's example to enliven
our Eucharistic spirit in daily life.*

Saint John Paul II said, "Mary is a woman of the Eucharist in her whole life."[33] Through Baptism, each of us has been deeply associated to the mystery of Jesus' saving life, passion, death, and Resurrection, which is memorialized every time we celebrate the Eucharist. Saint John Paul II reminded us that every follower of Christ is called to be, like Mary, a woman or man of the Eucharist.

Prayer of Adoration

Jesus, present everywhere,
But uniquely here in the Blessed Sacrament,
in this gift of your self-giving love,
we adore you
and we ask you to make us men and women of
    the Eucharist.

Immerse us in your paschal mystery,
and help us to say "yes"
to your invitation to participate in your life
and self-offering.

Adoring Jesus Truth

In the wedding at Cana, Mary's heart beats so closely with that of her Son that she anticipates his desire and action. The wedding feast, with its miraculous abundance of flowing wine, prefigures the Eucharistic banquet in which Jesus gives us his own Body and Blood, a sharing in his abundant life. Especially noteworthy is Mary's response of faith when Jesus appears to refuse her request.

Reading: John 2:1–11

On the third day there was a wedding in Cana of Galilee, and the mother of Jesus was there. Jesus and his disciples had also been invited to the wedding. When the wine gave out, the mother of Jesus said to him, "They have no wine." And Jesus said to her, "Woman, what concern is that to you and to me? My hour has not yet come." His mother said to the servants, "Do whatever he tells you." Now standing there were six stone water-jars for the Jewish rites of purification, each holding twenty or thirty gallons. Jesus said to them, "Fill the jars with water." And they filled them up to the brim. He said to them, "Now draw some out, and take it to the chief steward." So they took it. When the steward tasted the water that had become wine, and did not know where it came from (though the servants who had drawn the water knew), the steward called the bridegroom and said to him, "Everyone serves the good wine first, and then the inferior wine after the guests have become drunk. But you have kept the good wine until now." Jesus did this, the first of his signs, in Cana of Galilee, and revealed his glory; and his disciples believed in him.

Reflection

Mary's deep faith is clearly expressed in her ability to trust in her divine Son, even when he *seems* indifferent to the situation. She models the kind of faith all of us need in our lives, when we wonder how God is at work in the difficulties we face. Like Mary, you are called to go beyond intellectual belief. A deep belief in the physical presence of Jesus in the Eucharist entails being convinced that Jesus' saving love is at work in our world, no matter how hidden: in the Eucharist certainly, also within you, in others, in the Church, in your life situations right now.

At each Eucharistic Celebration when Jesus pours himself out for love of you, he asks you, "Do this in remembrance of me." In this appeal, Jesus invites you to receive the abundant gift of his life; he also invites you, in turn, to share that same life with others. And this is perhaps the deepest act of faith: to discover how you are called to be the loving presence of Jesus for others.

To give fully of yourself means loving others to the point of self-forgetfulness and self-sacrifice. It means sharing in the same love that Jesus has for your brothers and sisters. How might Jesus be asking you to participate more fully in the life-giving mystery of his suffering, death, and Resurrection?

You can offer yourself to Jesus, to be united with him and to experience his self-giving love more fully:

Jesus Master,
I offer my entire being to you;
I open myself to your love
and ask the Holy Spirit to gradually transform me.
May my communion with you
develop in me a capacity for love
which empowers me to be sensitive to others,
and strengthened for self-giving and continual adaptation.
May this love make me creative, dynamic, and deeply committed
to do something for the Lord and for the people of this time.[34]

Following Jesus Way

Mary's Canticle, the Magnificat, is a prayer of praise and thanksgiving, recalling the saving works of God, particularly the redemptive Incarnation. Mary's Canticle also reflects a Eucharistic attitude:

Every time the Son of God comes again to us in the "poverty" of the sacramental signs of bread and wine, the seeds of that new history wherein the mighty are "put down from their thrones" and "those of low degree are exalted" takes root in the world.[35]

Pray the Magnificat (see page 178), in the joyful light of Jesus' saving love for you.

Like no other person, Mary participated in Jesus' self-offering on Calvary. At the very moment of the worst possible suffering in her life, as she watched the cruel torture and execution of her beloved Son, Jesus asked her to unite her sacrifice to his and thus become the Mother of the Church and of all humanity. (See Jn 19:26–27.)

Reflect on how Jesus is calling you to participate in his paschal mystery in the situations and challenges in your life that you find difficult. When have you hesitated to love selflessly? How can Mary's generous "yes" to her Son, even on Calvary, inspire you?

Ask Jesus for forgiveness and mercy for the times and ways you have been afraid or resisted entering more deeply into the paschal mystery with the prayer To Jesus Crucified (see page 235).

Ask Mary to help you to live a Eucharistic life in this prayer inspired by Chapter 6 of *On the Eucharist in Its Relationship to the Church*:

Mary, we entrust our journey to you.
You abandoned yourself into the loving hands of God,

trusting God to work powerfully in your life:
"Behold the handmaid of the Lord."
May our faith in the Lord's Incarnation and Redemption
 be as complete as yours.
You adored the Son of God in your womb,
became a "living tabernacle"
in which your Son was adored by Elizabeth.
May our voices, eyes, and lives radiate his light.
You were with your Son on Calvary,
uniting yourself with your Son's self-giving love.
Help us to discover our place at the foot of the Cross,
and how we can give of ourselves more fully in love to our
 brothers and sisters.
You shared most wonderfully in the joy of Jesus'
 Resurrection.
help us to allow Jesus' promise of new life to transform
 our lives.
May we recognize the many ways your Son remains
 with us now,
and build a communion of love wherever he is present:
in the Church, in the Eucharist, in our families, with
 each person.
May we live fully the joy, awe, and delight that this
 Mystery of Love inspires!

Sharing Jesus' Life

Mary was so closely united to her Son that his prayer became her prayer. In chapter 17 of John's Gospel, at the Last Supper, Jesus prays urgently to the Father on our behalf. In this first Eucharistic prayer, Jesus prays for his followers, for us, for our union with him, and for our union with each other. Let us make this prayer of Jesus our own, asking Mary to help us unite our hearts to her Son's. (Jesus' Priestly Prayer begins on page 179.)

As you conclude your hour of adoration, make a spiritual communion (see page 43). Ask Mary, Mother of the Church, to help you choose a practical way to build unity sometime in the coming week: perhaps reconciling with someone who has offended or hurt you or beginning an activity that might help to bring family members closer together.

Part Four

Treasury of Prayers

If we really love the good God, we will find it a joy and happiness to spend some time near him, to adore him, and keep company with so good a friend. He is there in the tabernacle. What is Jesus doing, in this Sacrament of love? He is loving us.

—Saint John Vianney

Praying with the Bible

> Holy Scripture will be our most prized reading;
> this letter from our heavenly Father
> invites us to heaven,
> communicating to us his secrets,
> his most lovable truths,
> his designs for us.
>
> —Blessed James Alberione

The Beauty and Power of God's Word

In the library of books contained in the Bible, God reveals himself, the purpose of our existence, and the way to true happiness. Isn't this reason enough to find a Bible and open it? Yet, many of us don't open the Bible because we are too unfamiliar with it or intimidated by it.

Psalm 119 eloquently portrays the word of God as:

life-giving,
comforting,
precious,
a promise,
a song,

> a delight,
> giving understanding,
> a lamp or light,
> joy of our hearts,
> our hope,
> our safety.

We all want the life, comfort, treasure, promise, strength, and joy that reading and praying with the word of God can give. Because the Bible *is* the very word of God, it is active whenever we encounter it. God *always* speaks to us through his word.

God's word is one of the privileged, sure ways that we can get to know God's heart. By hearing God's desires and designs for us, we can truly come to know God.

Prayerfully Listening to God's Word

For many people, the Bible is an untapped treasure that needs to be unlocked with a secret key. There *is* a secret key to praying with the Bible, and it is this: knowing that God *wants* to communicate with us.

Because the Bible is God's word to us, we only need to open our hearts and truly listen. Not a passive "just being there," but a listening that is thirsty, that hangs on every syllable; a listening as eager as that of those in love who wait to catch the first whispered affirmations of their beloved's love.

Don't be afraid to slow down, read, and listen in a way that is truly receptive to God's invitational message of love: "You are precious to me," "I love you," "Remain in me," "Rest in me," "Follow me," "Seek first the kingdom of God," etc.

However you decide to read, study, and pray with the word of God, what is most important is to be open and let it shape your life, attitudes, and prayer. The biblical prayers included here are just a small selection of some of the most familiar. Your Bible is the best possible resource you can bring to your prayer before Jesus in the Holy Eucharist.

Blessed James Alberione believed that praying with the Bible before the Blessed Sacrament brought special graces and that the word of God and the Eucharist should be inseparable in our hearts.

> The Bible . . .
> is the great sacrament of God's word.
> Within its pages
> the divine fire of the Holy Spirit burns,
> just as under the sacramental species
> the divine Person of Christ lives.
> And just as the person
> who receives the Host
> is nourished by divine food that gives
> a strength unequalled by any other,
> so too the person who is nourished
> by the words of the Bible

experiences interiorly
the kindling of a divine fire
which causes an activity
that cannot be expressed,
one which pervades his or her being
and spiritually renews it.

The person who eats the Bread of Life
will live eternally.
When we nourish ourselves
on the word of the Bible
with the right dispositions,
we will be permeated by the Holy Spirit.[36]

Biblical Prayers

Psalm 23

The LORD is my shepherd; I shall not want.
>   He makes me lie down in green pastures.
> He leads me beside still waters.
>   He restores my soul.
> He leads me in paths of righteousness
>   for his name's sake.

Even though I walk through the valley of the shadow of death,
>   I will fear no evil,
> for you are with me;
>   your rod and your staff,
>   they comfort me.

You prepare a table before me
>   in the presence of my enemies;
> you anoint my head with oil;
>   my cup overflows.
> Surely goodness and mercy shall follow me
>   all the days of my life,
> and I shall dwell in the house of the Lord forever.

Psalm 31

In you, O Lord, do I take refuge;
>let me never be put to shame;
>in your righteousness deliver me!

Incline your ear to me;
>rescue me speedily!

Be a rock of refuge for me,
>a strong fortress to save me!

For you are my rock and my fortress;
>and for your name's sake you lead me and guide me;

you take me out of the net they have hidden for me,
>for you are my refuge.

Into your hand I commit my spirit;
>you have redeemed me, O Lord, faithful God.

I hate those who pay regard to worthless idols,
>but I trust in the Lord.

I will rejoice and be glad in your steadfast love,
>because you have seen my affliction;
>you have known the distress of my soul,

and you have not delivered me into the hand
>of the enemy;
>you have set my feet in a broad place.

Be gracious to me, O Lord, for I am in distress;
>my eye is wasted from grief;

my soul and my body also.
For my life is spent with sorrow,
>   and my years with sighing;
my strength fails because of my iniquity,
>   and my bones waste away.

Because of all my adversaries I have become a reproach,
>   especially to my neighbors,
and an object of dread to my acquaintances;
>   those who see me in the street flee from me.
I have been forgotten like one who is dead;
>   I have become like a broken vessel.
For I hear the whispering of many—
>   terror on every side!—
as they scheme together against me,
>   as they plot to take my life.

But I trust in you, O Lord;
>   I say, "You are my God."
My times are in your hand;
>   rescue me from the hand of my enemies and from my persecutors!
Make your face shine on your servant;
>   save me in your steadfast love!

Psalm 51

Have mercy on me, O God,
>according to your steadfast love;
according to your abundant mercy
>blot out my transgressions.
Wash me thoroughly from my iniquity,
>and cleanse me from my sin!

For I know my transgressions,
>and my sin is ever before me.
Against you, you only, have I sinned
>and done what is evil in your sight,
so that you may be justified in your words
>and blameless in your judgment.
Behold, I was brought forth in iniquity,
>and in sin did my mother conceive me.
Behold, you delight in truth in the inward being,
>and you teach me wisdom in the secret heart.

Purge me with hyssop, and I shall be clean;
>wash me, and I shall be whiter than snow.
Let me hear joy and gladness;
>let the bones that you have broken rejoice.
Hide your face from my sins,
>and blot out all my iniquities.
Create in me a clean heart, O God,
>and renew a right spirit within me.

Cast me not away from your presence,
    and take not your Holy Spirit from me.
Restore to me the joy of your salvation,
    and uphold me with a willing spirit.

Then I will teach transgressors your ways,
    and sinners will return to you.
Deliver me from bloodguiltiness, O God,
    O God of my salvation,
    and my tongue will sing aloud of your righteousness.
O Lord, open my lips,
    and my mouth will declare your praise.
For you will not delight in sacrifice, or I would give it;
    you will not be pleased with a burnt offering.
The sacrifices of God are a broken spirit;
    a broken and contrite heart, O God, you will not despise.

Do good to Zion in your good pleasure;
    build up the walls of Jerusalem;
then will you delight in right sacrifices,
    in burnt offerings and whole burnt offerings;
    then bulls will be offered on your altar.

Psalm 63

O God, you are my God; earnestly I seek you;
  my soul thirsts for you;
my flesh faints for you,
  as in a dry and weary land where there is no water.
So I have looked upon you in the sanctuary,
  beholding your power and glory.
Because your steadfast love is better than life,
  my lips will praise you.
So I will bless you as long as I live;
  in your name I will lift up my hands.

My soul will be satisfied as with fat and rich food,
  and my mouth will praise you with joyful lips,
when I remember you upon my bed,
  and meditate on you in the watches of the night;
for you have been my help,
  and in the shadow of your wings I will sing for joy.
My soul clings to you;
  your right hand upholds me.

Psalm 100

Make a joyful noise to the LORD, all the earth!
    Serve the LORD with gladness!
    Come into his presence with singing!

Know that the LORD, he is God!
    It is he who made us, and we are his;
    we are his people, and the sheep of his pasture.

Enter his gates with thanksgiving,
    and his courts with praise!
    Give thanks to him; bless his name!

For the LORD is good;
    his steadfast love endures forever,
    and his faithfulness to all generations.

Psalm 116

I love the LORD, because he has heard
    my voice and my pleas for mercy.
Because he inclined his ear to me,
    therefore I will call on him as long as I live.
The snares of death encompassed me;
    the pangs of Sheol laid hold on me;
    I suffered distress and anguish.
Then I called on the name of the LORD:
    "O LORD, I pray, deliver my soul!"

Gracious is the LORD, and righteous;
>   our God is merciful.
The LORD preserves the simple;
>   when I was brought low, he saved me.
Return, O my soul, to your rest;
>   for the LORD has dealt bountifully with you.

For you have delivered my soul from death,
>   my eyes from tears,
>   my feet from stumbling;
I will walk before the LORD
>   in the land of the living.

I believed, even when I spoke:
>   "I am greatly afflicted";
I said in my alarm,
>   "All mankind are liars."

What shall I render to the LORD
>   for all his benefits to me?
I will lift up the cup of salvation
>   and call on the name of the LORD,
I will pay my vows to the LORD
>   in the presence of all his people.

Precious in the sight of the LORD
>   is the death of his saints.
O LORD, I am your servant;
>   I am your servant, the son of your maidservant.
>   You have loosed my bonds.

I will offer to you the sacrifice of thanksgiving
    and call on the name of the LORD.
I will pay my vows to the LORD
    in the presence of all his people,
in the courts of the house of the LORD,
    in your midst, O Jerusalem.
Praise the LORD!

Psalm 118

Oh give thanks to the LORD, for he is good;
    for his steadfast love endures forever!

Let Israel say,
    "His steadfast love endures forever."
Let the house of Aaron say,
    "His steadfast love endures forever."
Let those who fear the LORD say,
    "His steadfast love endures forever."

Out of my distress I called on the LORD;
    the LORD answered me and set me free.
The LORD is on my side; I will not fear.
    What can man do to me?
The LORD is on my side as my helper;
    I shall look in triumph on those who hate me.

It is better to take refuge in the LORD
    than to trust in man.

It is better to take refuge in the LORD
  than to trust in princes.

All nations surrounded me;
  in the name of the LORD I cut them off!
They surrounded me, surrounded me on every side;
  in the name of the LORD I cut them off!
They surrounded me like bees;
  they went out like a fire among thorns;
  in the name of the LORD I cut them off!
I was pushed hard, so that I was falling,
  but the LORD helped me.

The LORD is my strength and my song;
  he has become my salvation.
Glad songs of salvation
  are in the tents of the righteous:
"The right hand of the LORD does valiantly,
  the right hand of the LORD exalts,
  the right hand of the LORD does valiantly!"

I shall not die, but I shall live,
  and recount the deeds of the LORD.
The LORD has disciplined me severely,
  but he has not given me over to death.

Open to me the gates of righteousness,
  that I may enter through them
  and give thanks to the LORD.

This is the gate of the LORD;
    the righteous shall enter through it.
I thank you that you have answered me
    and have become my salvation.
The stone that the builders rejected
    has become the cornerstone.
This is the LORD's doing;
    it is marvelous in our eyes.
This is the day that the LORD has made;
    let us rejoice and be glad in it.

Save us, we pray, O LORD!
    O LORD, we pray, give us success!

Blessed is he who comes in the name of the LORD!
    We bless you from the house of the LORD.
    The LORD is God,
    and he has made his light to shine upon us.
    Bind the festal sacrifice with cords,
    up to the horns of the altar!

You are my God, and I will give thanks to you;
    you are my God; I will extol you.
Oh give thanks to the LORD, for he is good;
    for his steadfast love endures forever!

Psalm 130

Out of the depths I cry to you, O Lord!
> O Lord, hear my voice!
Let your ears be attentive
> to the voice of my pleas for mercy!

If you, O Lord, should mark iniquities,
> O Lord, who could stand?
But with you there is forgiveness,
> that you may be feared.

I wait for the Lord, my soul waits,
> and in his word I hope;
my soul waits for the Lord
> more than watchmen for the morning,
> more than watchmen for the morning.

O Israel, hope in the Lord!
> For with the Lord there is steadfast love,
> and with him is plentiful redemption.
And he will redeem Israel
> from all his iniquities.

Psalm 139

O Lord, you have searched me and known me!
You know when I sit down and when I rise up;
> you discern my thoughts from afar.

You search out my path and my lying down
    and are acquainted with all my ways.
Even before a word is on my tongue,
    behold, O LORD, you know it altogether.
You hem me in, behind and before,
    and lay your hand upon me.
Such knowledge is too wonderful for me;
    it is high; I cannot attain it.

Where shall I go from your Spirit?
    Or where shall I flee from your presence?
If I ascend to heaven, you are there!
    If I make my bed in Sheol, you are there!
If I take the wings of the morning
    and dwell in the uttermost parts of the sea,
even there your hand shall lead me,
    and your right hand shall hold me.
If I say, "Surely the darkness shall cover me,
    and the light about me be night,"
even the darkness is not dark to you;
    the night is bright as the day,
    for darkness is as light with you.

For you formed my inward parts;
    you knitted me together in my mother's womb.
I praise you, for I am fearfully and wonderfully made.
Wonderful are your works;
    my soul knows it very well.

My frame was not hidden from you,
when I was being made in secret,
>> intricately woven in the depths of the earth.
Your eyes saw my unformed substance;
in your book were written, every one of them,
>> the days that were formed for me,
>> when as yet there was none of them.

How precious to me are your thoughts, O God!
>> How vast is the sum of them!
If I would count them, they are more than the sand.
>> I awake, and I am still with you.

Oh that you would slay the wicked, O God!
>> O men of blood, depart from me!
They speak against you with malicious intent;
>> your enemies take your name in vain.
Do I not hate those who hate you, O LORD?
>> And do I not loathe those who rise up against you?
I hate them with complete hatred;
>> I count them my enemies.

Search me, O God, and know my heart!
>> Try me and know my thoughts!
And see if there be any grievous way in me,
>> and lead me in the way everlasting!

Canticle of Isaiah 55

Come, everyone who thirsts,
>come to the waters;
and he who has no money,
>come, buy and eat!
Come, buy wine and milk
>without money and without price.
Why do you spend your money for that which
>is not bread,
>and your labor for that which does not satisfy?
Listen diligently to me, and eat what is good,
>and delight yourselves in rich food.
Incline your ear, and come to me;
>hear, that your soul may live;
and I will make with you an everlasting covenant,
>my steadfast, sure love for David.
Behold, I made him a witness to the peoples,
>a leader and commander for the peoples.
Behold, you shall call a nation that you do not know,
>and a nation that did not know you shall run to you,
because of the LORD your God, and of the Holy One
>>of Israel,
>for he has glorified you.

Seek the LORD while he may be found;
>call upon him while he is near;
let the wicked forsake his way,

and the unrighteous man his thoughts;
let him return to the LORD, that he may have compassion
    on him,
and to our God, for he will abundantly pardon.
For my thoughts are not your thoughts,
    neither are your ways my ways, declares the LORD.
For as the heavens are higher than the earth,
    so are my ways higher than your ways
    and my thoughts than your thoughts.

For as the rain and the snow come down from heaven
    and do not return there but water the earth,
making it bring forth and sprout,
    giving seed to the sower and bread to the eater,
so shall my word be that goes out from my mouth;
    it shall not return to me empty,
but it shall accomplish that which I purpose,
    and shall succeed in the thing for which I sent it.

For you shall go out in joy
    and be led forth in peace;
the mountains and the hills before you
    shall break forth into singing,
    and all the trees of the field shall clap their hands.
Instead of the thorn shall come up the cypress;
    instead of the brier shall come up the myrtle;
and it shall make a name for the LORD,
    an everlasting sign that shall not be cut off.

Benedictus

Blessed be the Lord God of Israel,
> for he has visited and redeemed his people
and has raised up a horn of salvation for us
> in the house of his servant David,
as he spoke by the mouth of his holy prophets
> from of old,
that we should be saved from our enemies
> and from the hand of all who hate us;
to show the mercy promised to our fathers
> and to remember his holy covenant,
the oath that he swore to our father Abraham, to grant us
> that we, being delivered from the hand of our enemies,
might serve him without fear,
> in holiness and righteousness before him all our days.
And you, child, will be called the prophet of the Most High;
> for you will go before the Lord to prepare his ways,
to give knowledge of salvation to his people
> in the forgiveness of their sins,
because of the tender mercy of our God,
> whereby the sunrise shall visit us from on high
to give light to those who sit in darkness and in the shadow of death,
> to guide our feet into the way of peace.

Luke 1:68–79

Magnificat

My soul magnifies the Lord,
> and my spirit rejoices in God my Savior,

for he has looked on the humble estate of his servant.
> For behold, from now on all generations will call me blessed;

for he who is mighty has done great things for me,
> and holy is his name.

And his mercy is for those who fear him
> from generation to generation.

He has shown strength with his arm;
> he has scattered the proud in the thoughts of their hearts;

he has brought down the mighty from their thrones
> and exalted those of humble estate;

he has filled the hungry with good things,
> and the rich he has sent away empty.

He has helped his servant Israel,
> in remembrance of his mercy,

as he spoke to our fathers,
> to Abraham and to his offspring forever.

Luke 1:46–55

Jesus' Priestly Prayer

"Father, the hour has come; glorify your Son so that the Son may glorify you, since you have given him authority over all people, to give eternal life to all whom you have given him. And this is eternal life, that they may know you, the only true God, and Jesus Christ whom you have sent. I glorified you on earth by finishing the work that you gave me to do. So now, Father, glorify me in your own presence with the glory that I had in your presence before the world existed.

"I have made your name known to those whom you gave me from the world. They were yours, and you gave them to me, and they have kept your word. Now they know that everything you have given me is from you; for the words that you gave to me I have given to them, and they have received them and know in truth that I came from you; and they have believed that you sent me. I am asking on their behalf; I am not asking on behalf of the world, but on behalf of those whom you gave me, because they are yours. All mine are yours, and yours are mine; and I have been glorified in them. And now I am no longer in the world, but they are in the world, and I am coming to you. Holy Father, protect them in your name that you have given me, so that they may be one, as we are one. While I was with them, I protected them in your name that you have given me. I guarded them, and not one of them was lost except the one destined to be lost, so that the scripture might be fulfilled. But now I am coming to you, and

I speak these things in the world so that they may have my joy made complete in themselves. I have given them your word, and the world has hated them because they do not belong to the world, just as I do not belong to the world. I am not asking you to take them out of the world, but I ask you to protect them from the evil one. They do not belong to the world, just as I do not belong to the world. Sanctify them in the truth; your word is truth. As you have sent me into the world, so I have sent them into the world. And for their sakes I sanctify myself, so that they also may be sanctified in truth.

"I ask not only on behalf of these, but also on behalf of those who will believe in me through their word, that they may all be one. As you, Father, are in me and I am in you, may they also be in us, so that the world may believe that you have sent me. The glory that you have given me I have given them, so that they may be one, as we are one, I in them and you in me, that they may become completely one, so that the world may know that you have sent me and have loved them even as you have loved me. Father, I desire that those also, whom you have given me, may be with me where I am, to see my glory, which you have given me because you loved me before the foundation of the world.

"Righteous Father, the world does not know you, but I know you; and these know that you have sent me. I made your name known to them, and I will make it known, so that the love with which you have loved me may be in them, and I in them."

John 17:1–26

Canticle of Ephesians 1

Blessed be the God and Father of our Lord Jesus Christ, who has blessed us in Christ with every spiritual blessing in the heavenly places, even as he chose us in him before the foundation of the world, that we should be holy and blameless before him. In love he predestined us for adoption to himself as sons through Jesus Christ, according to the purpose of his will, to the praise of his glorious grace, with which he has blessed us in the Beloved. In him we have redemption through his blood, the forgiveness of our trespasses, according to the riches of his grace, which he lavished upon us, in all wisdom and insight making known to us the mystery of his will, according to his purpose, which he set forth in Christ as a plan for the fullness of time, to unite all things in him, things in heaven and things on earth.

In him we have obtained an inheritance, having been predestined according to the purpose of him who works all things according to the counsel of his will, so that we who were the first to hope in Christ might be to the praise of his glory. In him you also, when you heard the word of truth, the gospel of your salvation, and believed in him, were sealed with the promised Holy Spirit, who is the guarantee of our inheritance until we acquire possession of it, to the praise of his glory.

Ephesians 1:3–14

Canticle of 1 Peter

Blessed be the God and Father of our Lord Jesus Christ! According to his great mercy, he has caused us to be born again to a living hope through the resurrection of Jesus Christ from the dead, to an inheritance that is imperishable, undefiled, and unfading, kept in heaven for you, who by God's power are being guarded through faith for a salvation ready to be revealed in the last time. In this you rejoice, though now for a little while, if necessary, you have been grieved by various trials, so that the tested genuineness of your faith—more precious than gold that perishes though it is tested by fire—may be found to result in praise and glory and honor at the revelation of Jesus Christ. Though you have not seen him, you love him. Though you do not now see him, you believe in him and rejoice with joy that is inexpressible and filled with glory, obtaining the outcome of your faith, the salvation of your souls.

1 Peter 1:3–9

Canticle of Revelation 19

*This Canticle is made up of excerpts from
the heavenly songs John hears.*

Hallelujah!
Salvation and glory and power belong to our God,
    for his judgments are true and just....

Hallelujah!
... Praise our God,
    all you his servants,
you who fear him,
    small and great....

Hallelujah!
For the Lord our God
    the Almighty reigns.
Let us rejoice and exult
    and give him the glory,
for the marriage of the Lamb has come,
    and his Bride has made herself ready.

Revelation 19:1–3, 5–7

Prayers of Adoration

Adoration is the foundation of our relationship with our Creator, the all-good, all-knowing, all-beautiful Lord. Adoration is wondering love: a spontaneous response to the God who loves us beyond our understanding.

What kind of response dare we give to the Almighty, who humbly and mysteriously gives himself to us in the Holy Eucharist?

Our awe, wonder, reverence, love, and delight—none are truly worthy of the Lord of heaven and earth, yet they are precious to God because they come from our hearts.

> May I never leave you there alone but be wholly present, my faith wholly vigilant, wholly adoring, and wholly surrendered to your creative action.
>
> —Saint Elizabeth of the Trinity

Morning Offering

The Morning Offering is a deeply Eucharistic prayer, setting the tone for the whole day.

Divine Heart of Jesus, through the Immaculate Heart of Mary, I offer you my prayers, works, joys, and sufferings of this day, for all the intentions of your Sacred Heart, in union with the Holy Sacrifice of the Mass throughout the world, for the salvation of souls, the reparation of sins, the reunion of all Christians, and for the intentions of the Holy Father recommended this month.

Prayer of Adoration

> Jesus, today's adoration is the meeting of my soul
> and my entire being with you.
> I am the creature meeting you, my Creator;
> the disciple before the Divine Master;
> the patient with the Doctor of souls;
> the poor one appealing to the Rich One;
> the thirsty one drinking at the Font;
> the weak one before the Almighty;
> the tempted seeking a sure Refuge;
> the blind person searching for the Light;
> the friend who goes to the True Friend;
> the lost sheep sought by the Divine Shepherd;
> the wayward heart who finds the Way;
> the unenlightened one who finds Wisdom;
> the bride who finds the Spouse of the soul;
> the "nothing" who finds the All;
> the afflicted who finds the Consoler;
> the seeker who finds life's meaning.

Adapted from Blessed James Alberione

Prayer of Presence

Lord, I come before you here in the Eucharist,
and believe that you are looking at me and listening
   to my prayer.
You are so great and so holy, I adore you.
You have given me everything, I thank you.
I have sinned against you, and I ask your pardon with a
   heart full of sorrow.
You are rich in mercy; I ask you to grant me all the graces
   that will help me draw closer to you.

You

You are the peace of all things calm.
You are the place to hide from harm.
You are the light that shines in the dark.
You are the heart's eternal spark.
You are the door that's open wide.
You are the guest who waits inside.
You are the stranger at the door.
You are the calling of the poor.
You are the light, the truth, the way.
You are my Savior this very day.

An Ancient Celtic Blessing

Chaplet to Jesus Master, Way, Truth, and Life

1. Jesus, Divine Master, we adore you as the Word Incarnate sent by the Father to instruct us in life-giving truths. You are uncreated Truth, the only Master. You alone have words of eternal life. We thank you for having imparted to us the light of reason and the light of faith, and for having called us to the light of glory. We believe, submitting our whole mind to you and to the Church. Master, show us the treasures of your wisdom, let us know the Father, make us your true disciples. Increase our faith so that we may attain to the eternal vision in heaven.

Jesus Master, Way, Truth, and Life, have mercy on us.

2. Jesus, Divine Master, we adore you as the Beloved of the Father, the sole Way to him. We thank you because you made yourself our model. You left us examples of the highest perfection. You have invited us to follow you on earth and in heaven. We contemplate you in the various periods of your earthly life. We docilely place ourselves in your school and follow your teachings. Draw us to you so that by following in your footsteps and renouncing ourselves, we may seek only your will. Increase active hope in us, the desire to be found similar to you at the judgment, and to possess you forever in heaven.

Jesus Master, Way, Truth, and Life, have mercy on us.

3. Jesus, Divine Master, we adore you as the only-begotten Son of God, come on the earth to give life, the most abundant life, to humanity. We thank you because by dying on the cross, you merited life for us, which you give us in Baptism and nourish in the Eucharist and in the other sacraments. Live in us, O Jesus, with the outpouring of the Holy Spirit, so that we may love you with our whole mind, strength, and heart, and love our neighbor as ourselves for love of you. Increase charity in us, so that one day, called from the sepulcher to the glorious life, we may be united with you in the eternal happiness of heaven.

Jesus Master, Way, Truth, and Life, have mercy on us.

4. Jesus, Divine Master, we adore you living in the Church, your Mystical Body and our sole ark of salvation. We thank you for having given us this infallible and indefectible Mother, in whom you continue to be for humanity the Way, the Truth, and the Life. We ask of you that those who do not believe may come to her inextinguishable light, the erring return to her, and all people be united in faith, in a common hope, in charity. Exalt the Church, assist the Pope, sanctify the clergy and those consecrated to you. Lord Jesus, our wish is yours: that there be one fold under one Shepherd, so that we may all be reunited in the Church exultant in heaven.

Jesus Master, Way, Truth, and Life, have mercy on us.

5. Jesus, Divine Master, we adore you with the angels who sang the reasons for your Incarnation: "Glory to God and peace to all people." We thank you for having called us to share in your own apostolate. Enkindle in us your own flame of zeal for God and for souls. Fill all our powers with yourself. Live in us so that we may radiate you through our apostolate of prayer and suffering, of the media and of the word, of example and of deed. Send good laborers into your harvest. Enlighten preachers, teachers, and writers; infuse in them the Holy Spirit with his seven gifts; dispose minds and hearts to receive him. Come, Master and Lord! Teach and reign through Mary, Mother, Teacher, and Queen.

Jesus Master, Way, Truth, and Life, have mercy on us.

Blessed James Alberione

Chaplet of Eucharistic Adoration

Make the Sign of the Cross and pray the Eucharistic prayer of the angel at Fatima:

Most Holy Trinity, I adore you! My God, I love you in the most Blessed Sacrament.

The chaplet can be prayed with or without beads. The chaplet beads are made up of one single bead, three beads, and then a circle of three sets of ten beads each time preceded by a single bead.

On the first single bead, pray:

I adore you, Eucharistic Jesus, present in so many tabernacles throughout the world. I unite myself to you in love, especially in those churches where you are abandoned and neglected.

On the three beads that follow, pray:

Jesus in the Holy Eucharist, you are eternal Truth; I believe in you.

Jesus in the Holy Eucharist, you are the Way of salvation; I hope in you.

Jesus in the Holy Eucharist, you are my Life; I love you with all my heart above all things and unite myself to you in the Blessed Sacrament.

On the centerpiece medal make an act of spiritual communion (see page 43).

On the single beads between the decades, pray:

Father, Son, and Holy Spirit, I praise and thank you for your great love manifest in your precious gift of the most Holy Eucharist; may it be known, honored, and adored by everyone.

On the sets of 10 beads, pray:

Eucharistic Jesus, my Way, Truth, and Life, truly present in the most Blessed Sacrament of the altar, I adore you, love you, and unite myself to you in all the tabernacles throughout the world.

Conclude the chaplet with the Divine Praises (see page 64).

Mary Leonora Wilson, FSP

Bread of My Soul

I place myself in the presence of him, in whose Incarnate Presence I am before I place myself there.

I adore you, my Savior, present here as God and man, in soul and Body, in true flesh and Blood.

I acknowledge and confess that I kneel before that sacred humanity, who was conceived in Mary's womb and lay in Mary's bosom; who grew up to man's estate, and by the Sea of Galilee called the Twelve, wrought miracles, and spoke words of wisdom and peace; who in due season hung on the cross, lay in the tomb, rose from the dead, and now reigns in heaven.

I praise, and bless, and give myself wholly to him, who is the true Bread of my soul, and my everlasting joy.

Saint John Henry Newman

Immersed in Adoration

I adore you, Lord and Creator, hidden in the Blessed Sacrament. I adore you for all the works of your hands that reveal to me so much wisdom, goodness, and mercy, O Lord. You have spread so much beauty over the earth, and it tells me about your beauty, even though these beautiful things are but a faint reflection of you, incomprehensible Beauty. And although you have hidden yourself and concealed your beauty, my eye, enlightened by faith, reaches you and I recognize my Creator, my highest Good, and my heart is completely immersed in prayer of adoration.

Saint Faustina Kowalska[37]

We Adore You

We adore you, most holy Lord Jesus Christ, here and in all your churches throughout the world. We bless you, because by your holy Cross you have redeemed the world.

Attributed to Saint Francis of Assisi

Beloved Jesus

Beloved Jesus, I believe that you are truly present here in the Eucharist. I adore you.

You look at me and listen to me as I look at you and listen to you. I love you.

You have given me everything that I am and have. Thank you.

Please open my heart and mind so that our visit together may be a time of union and love and that I may be transformed in you, my Teacher and Master. Amen.

Patricia Cora Shaules, FSP

Stay with Me, Lord

Stay with me, Lord, for it is necessary to have you present so that I do not forget you.

Stay with me, Lord, because I am weak and I need your strength, that I may not fall so often.

Stay with me, Lord, for you are my life, and without you, I am without fervor.

Stay with me, Lord, for you are my light, and without you, I am in darkness.

Stay with me, Lord, to show me your will.

Stay with me, Lord, so that I hear your voice and follow you.

Stay with me, Lord, for I desire to love you very much, and always be in your company.

Stay with me, Lord, if you wish me to be faithful to you.

Stay with me, Lord, for as poor as my soul is, I wish it to be a place of consolation for you, a nest of love...

Stay with me tonight, Jesus, in life with all its dangers, I need you.

Let me recognize you as your disciples did at the breaking of bread, so that Eucharistic Communion may be the light that disperses the darkness, the force that sustains me, the unique joy of my heart...

Stay with me, Lord, for it is you alone I look for. Your love, your grace, your will, your heart, your Spirit, because I love you and ask no other reward but to love you more and more.

With a firm love, I will love you with all my heart. Amen.

Saint Pio of Pietrelcina[38]

Act of Abandonment

You, O my God, always think of me.
You are within me, outside of me.
I am written on the palm of your hand.
O Lord, that I may always and in all things do your will.
O Lord, I abandon myself in you.
No worries.
I abandon myself completely in you, always.

Venerable Thecla Merlo, FSP

Act of Adoration

Jesus, my God, I adore you
here present in the Blessed Sacrament of the altar,
where you wait day and night to be our comfort while we await
your unveiled presence in heaven.

Jesus, my God, I adore you
in all places where the Blessed Sacrament is reserved,
and where sins are committed against this Sacrament of Love.

Jesus, my God, I adore you for all time,
past, present, and future,
for every soul that ever was, is, or shall be created.

Jesus, my God,
who for us endured hunger and cold, labor and fatigue,
I adore you.

Jesus, my God,
who for my sake deigned to subject yourself
to the humiliation of temptation,
to the betrayal and defection of friends,
to the scorn of your enemies,
I adore you.

Jesus, my God,
who for us endured the buffeting of your passion,
the scourging,

the crowning with thorns,
the heavy weight of the Cross,
I adore you.

Jesus, my God, who, for my salvation and that of
    the whole human race,
was cruelly nailed to the Cross
and hung there for three long hours in bitter agony,
I adore you.

Jesus, my God, who for love of us instituted this
    Blessed Sacrament
and offered your life for the sins of the whole world,
I adore you.

Jesus, my God,
who in Holy Communion became the food of my soul,
I adore you.

Jesus, for you I live.
Jesus, for you I die.
Jesus, I am all yours in life and death. Amen.

Cardinal John J. Carberry[39]

Litany of the Most Blessed Sacrament

This litany's descriptions of the Eucharist can move hearts to deeper adoration. Feel free to adapt the response from "have mercy on us," to something that appeals to you personally, such as "we adore you," "we love you," or "we trust in you."

Lord, have mercy on us. ℟. *Christ, have mercy on us.*
Lord, have mercy on us. Christ, hear us.
>   ℟. *Christ, graciously hear us.*

God, the Father of heaven, ℟. *have mercy on us.*

God the Son, Redeemer of the world, ℟.

God the Holy Spirit, ℟.

Holy Trinity, one God, ℟.

Jesus, living Bread come down from heaven, ℟.

Jesus, Bread from heaven giving life to the world, ℟.

Jesus, hidden God and Savior, ℟.

Jesus, who has loved us with an everlasting love, ℟.

Jesus, whose delight is to be with the children of men, ℟.

Jesus, who gave your flesh for the life of the world, ℟.

Jesus, who invites all to come to you, ℟.

Jesus, who promises eternal life to those who receive your Body and Blood, ℟.

Jesus, ever ready to welcome us to the table of the Eucharist, ℟.

Jesus, who stands knocking at the door of our hearts, ℟.

Jesus, who welcomes us and blesses us, ℟.

Jesus, who allows us to sit at your feet with Mary of Bethany, ℟.

Jesus, who invites us to follow you as your disciples, ℟.

Jesus, who has not left us orphans, ℟.

Sacrament of love, ℟.

Sacrament of all goodness, ℟.

Sacrament of strength, ℟.

Sacrament of nourishing grace, ℟.

That you reveal yourself to us in the breaking
 of bread as you did to the two disciples
 at Emmaus, ℟. *we beseech you, hear us.*

That you bless us who have not seen and yet
 have believed, ℟.

That we may love you with all our heart,
 all our soul, all our mind, and all our strength, ℟.

That the fruit of each Communion may be to love
 others for love of you, ℟.

That our one desire may be to love you and
 to do your will, ℟.

That we may forever remain in your love, ℟.

That you would teach us to pray as you taught
 your disciples, ℟.

That you grant us every virtue for right living, ℟.

That throughout this day you will keep us
 closely united to you, ℟.

That you give us the grace to persevere to the end, ℟.

That you be our comfort and support in our final hours, ℟.

That you deliver us safely into the arms of our
 heavenly Father, ℟.

Lamb of God, you take away the sins of the world,
spare us, O Lord.
Lamb of God, you take away the sins of the world,
graciously hear us, O Lord.
Lamb of God, you take away the sins of the world,
have mercy on us.

Let us pray.

Heavenly Father, you draw us to yourself through the wondrous Eucharistic mystery. Grant us a strong and lively faith in this Sacrament of love in which your Son Jesus Christ is present, offered, and received. We ask this through the same Christ our Lord. Amen.

Credo, Adoro, Amo

I Believe, I Adore, I Love

Credo: I believe, Lord, that you are truly, substantially present in the Blessed Sacrament: the same God incarnate who became like us in all things, except sin, and redeemed us by your supreme act of love on Calvary.

Credo: I believe. What else could I do? You have the words of eternal life: "Take this, all of you, and eat it; this is my Body. Take this, all of you, and drink from it; this is the cup of my Blood, the Blood of the new and everlasting covenant. It will be shed for you and for all so that sins may be forgiven."

Credo: I believe, Lord, increase my faith.

Adoro: I adore you, Lord, the Alpha and the Omega, the Beginning and the End of my life, without whose Divine Providence I could not draw a breath or move a limb.

All that I am, all that I have, I owe to you. Without you I am nothing and can do nothing. You are my God and my all. Help me to be totally dedicated to you.

I offer myself as your hands and feet to run errands of charity in your name. Yes, I give myself to you as a living tool in your hands—as your servant, if need be.

Adoro: I adore you, O Lord, with every fiber of my being.

Amo: I love you, O Lord, with my whole heart and soul, not for what you will give me but for what you are—Infinite Love. If I cannot love you with the immaculate love of your Blessed Mother, give me the grace to love you with the penitent heart of a Magdalen. If I cannot love you with the angelic love of a Saint John, give me the grace to love you with the penitent heart of a Peter.

Amo: I love you, O Lord, with my whole heart and soul.

Richard Cardinal Cushing

Loving Lord, I Believe

Loving Lord, I believe that you are truly present—Body, Blood, soul, and divinity—in the most Holy Eucharist. I adore you dwelling in the tabernacle, waiting for me to spend time with you, waiting to share yourself and your many graces with me and with all who approach you. You are the Living Bread come down from heaven; I praise you for this tremendous gift! Nourish me with your Body and your word. Increase my faith and inflame my heart with burning love for you. Remain with me and strengthen me on my pilgrim way; transform my thoughts, words, and deeds into signs of your presence for everyone whose life I touch today.

Mary Leonora Wilson, FSP

Prayer Before the Blessed Sacrament

Jesus, my Lord and my God, Creator and Ruler of the universe, I lovingly adore you, hidden so humbly beneath the appearance of the fragile Host. I am in awe to reflect that as I kneel before the Blessed Sacrament, I am not venerating a relic but worshipping the infinite God. I rejoice that the Blessed Sacrament is not merely a holy thing but a living Person—the same Christ who died on Calvary for each and every one of us, but who loved us so much that he wanted to remain with us forever.

Dear sacramental Savior, when you rose gloriously from the tomb you showed your infinite power, but when you remain silently in the tabernacle you show your infinite love.

Like the Wise Men who worshipped you in Bethlehem under a dazzling star, I adore you under the soft glow of the sanctuary lamp during this Eucharistic hour. I cannot bring you the gifts of the Magi, but I lay at your feet my heart and soul, my very life.

Bless our Holy Father, the Pope, and the Church throughout the world. Bless those who suffer persecution for your sake, and those who preach your Gospel in distant lands. Bless our priests, our religious sisters and brothers, and increase their numbers. Bless my family and my dear departed loved ones, the sick and the homebound, those who have wandered from your fold and those who are searching for the truth.

You were my First Communion; be also the Viaticum of my old age. But in between, may you ever be my daily Bread, so that Holy Communion here on earth may be for me a sweet foretaste of an eternal union with you in heaven. Amen.

Richard Cardinal Cushing

Prayers of Praise and Thanksgiving

God doesn't need our praise or gratitude, but in offering them, our prayer is transformed.

Gratitude shifts our focus from ourselves and what we lack to God's abundant goodness. Remembering how God has loved and blessed us, we grow in faith, trusting God in all things.

Praise moves our hearts a step further, so that we focus not only on God's blessings, but also on God's very self. The Eucharist is the perfect prayer and the sacrifice of praise.

> Blessed be the Father, Son, and Holy Spirit for every second that the Heart of Jesus is with us in each and every tabernacle on earth. Blessed be Emmanuel—God with us!
>
> —Saint Manuel González García[40]

> God is bread when you're hungry. God is water when you're thirsty. God is a shelter from the storm. God is rest when you're weary. God's my doctor. God's my lawyer. God's my captain who never lost a battle. God is my lily of the valley.
>
> —Servant of God Thea Bowman

O Sacrament Most Holy

O Sacrament most holy, O Sacrament divine!
All praise and all thanksgiving be every moment thine!

May the Heart of Jesus

May the Heart of Jesus in the most Blessed Sacrament be praised, adored, and loved with grateful affection at every moment, in all the tabernacles of the world, even to the end of time. Amen.

Thanks Be to Thee

Thanks be to thee, my Lord Jesus Christ,
for all the benefits
which thou hast given me,
O most merciful Friend,
Redeemer,
Brother.
May I see thee more clearly,
love thee more dearly and
follow thee more nearly.

Saint Richard of Chichester

You Have First Loved Me

I adore you, Jesus, true God and true man, present here in the Holy Eucharist. United in spirit with all the faithful on earth and all the saints in heaven, I humbly kneel before you, in deepest gratitude for so great a blessing. I love you, my Jesus, with my whole heart, for you have first loved me.

May I never offend you by my lack of love. May your Eucharistic presence completely refresh me and lead me toward heaven. Mary, Mother of our Eucharistic Lord, pray for me and obtain for me a greater love for Jesus in the Eucharist. Amen.

Filled with Wonder

O Treasure of the poor! How marvelously you sustain souls, showing the abundance of your riches to them not all at once, but little by little. When I behold your great Majesty hidden beneath so slight a Host, I am filled with wonder. . . . I know not how our Lord gives me the strength and courage necessary to draw near to him, except that he who has had, and still has, such compassion on me, gives me strength. . . . How can I open my mouth, that has uttered so many words against him, to receive that most glorious Body, purity and compassion itself? The love that is visible in his most beautiful face, sweet and tender, pains and distresses the soul because it has not served him.

Saint Teresa of Avila

Forever Yours

Father,
you have given us infinity
and all things flow from your hands—
from the vast reaches of the galaxies
to the smallest grains of sand.
All creation chants your praise
in silence, sight, and sound adore!
Cradled in the arms of your embrace:
We are forever yours.

Jesus,
when our sins shrouded us in shadows
our eyes beheld despair.
We spurned all signs of your love below—
you, the fullness of God's care.
Yet you drew us to your embrace—
upon the Cross our hope restored.
Lifted in the light of your loving gaze:
We are forever yours.

Holy Spirit,
hidden guide dwelling deep within the soul,
wordlessly you awaken the thirst
for that home where the broken are made whole.
As calm covers the crashing surf
we yield to your embrace;

as you beacon us to safe harbor
in the intimacy of your grace:
We are forever yours.

Body of Christ,
we hold this awesome, boundless treasure
to be poured out on the world.
Behold these gifts of splendor—
his precious, priceless pearls!
And with our lives we trace
the pattern of God's love so all will know
the infinite riches of his grace.
We are forever yours.

Bernadette M. Reis, FSP

Te Deum

We praise you, O God,
we acclaim you as Lord;
all creation worships you,
the Father everlasting.
To you all angels, all the powers of heaven,
the cherubim and seraphim, sing in endless praise:
Holy, holy, holy Lord, God of power and might,
heaven and earth are full of your glory.
The glorious company of apostles praise you.
The noble fellowship of prophets praise you.

The white-robed army of martyrs praise you.
Throughout the world the holy Church acclaims you:
Father, of majesty unbounded,
your true and only Son, worthy of all praise,
the Holy Spirit, advocate and guide.
You, Christ, are the King of glory,
the eternal Son of the Father.
When you took our flesh to set us free
you humbly chose the Virgin's womb.
You overcame the sting of death
and opened the kingdom of heaven to all believers.
You are seated at God's right hand in glory.
We believe that you will come to be our judge.
Come then, Lord, and help your people,
bought with the price of your own Blood,
and bring us with your saints
to glory everlasting.

℣. Save your people, Lord, and bless your inheritance.
℟. Govern and uphold them now and always.

℣. Day by day we bless you.
℟. We praise your name forever.

℣. Keep us today, Lord, from all sin.
℟. Have mercy on us, Lord, have mercy.

℣. Lord, show us your love and mercy,
℟. for we have put our trust in you.

℣. In you, Lord, is our hope:
℟. let us never be put to shame.

Novena of Grace

We give you thanks, O Lord, for all your wondrous gifts.

We thank you for the gift of life: you called us into being so that we might be your children and live with you forever.

We thank you for our Baptism: you sealed us with the Holy Spirit, gifted us with your own life, grafted us into the Mystical Body of your divine Son.

We thank you for our vocation to join with the risen Christ in working to save and sanctify the world in which we live.

We thank you for this Eucharist: you have fed us on the Bread of Life, strengthened our faith, renewed our hope, deepened our love, made us one with one another in the Body of Christ, our Lord.

We give you thanks, O Lord, for all your wondrous gifts. Amen.

Michael Harter, SJ

A Grateful Heart

Thou hast given so much to me,
Give one thing more—a grateful heart;
Not thankful when it pleaseth me,

As if thy blessings had spare days;
But such a heart, whose pulse may be
Thy praise.

George Herbert

O Immense Love!

O my God, my true and only Love, what more could you have done to win my love? It wasn't enough for you to die for me, you instituted the Blessed Sacrament to make yourself my food, that you might give yourself entirely to me, your creature.

O immense Love! A God who gives himself totally to me! O my infinitely lovable God, I love you above all else, with all my heart.... In Communion you give yourself completely to me; now I give myself completely to you.

Saint Alphonsus de Liguori

Prayer of Thanksgiving

O Jesus, eternal God, thank you for your countless graces and blessings. Let every beat of my heart be a new hymn of thanksgiving to you, O God. Let every drop of my blood circulate for you, Lord. My soul is one hymn in adoration of your mercy. I love you, God, for yourself alone.

Saint Faustina Kowalska[41]

Praise of God's Love

Lord, you loved me from all eternity, therefore you created me.
You loved me after you had made me, therefore you became man for me.
You loved me after you became man for me, therefore you lived and died for me.
You loved me after you had died for me, therefore you rose again for me.
You loved me after you had risen for me, therefore you went to prepare a place for me.
You loved me after you had gone to prepare a place for me, therefore you came back to me.
You loved me after you had come back to me, therefore you desire to enter into me and be united with me.
This is the meaning of the Eucharist, the mystery of love. Amen.

Alban Goodier, SJ

Litany of the Eucharist

To make this litany even more a prayer of praise, feel free to change the petition, "have mercy on us," to: "we praise and adore you!"

Lord, have mercy. ℟. *Lord, have mercy.*
Christ, have mercy. ℟. *Christ, have mercy.*
Lord, have mercy. ℟. *Lord, have mercy.*

Jesus, the Most High, ℟. *have mercy on us.*

Jesus, the holy One, ℟.

Jesus, Word of God, ℟.

Jesus, only Son of the Father, ℟.

Jesus, Son of Mary, ℟.

Jesus, crucified for us, ℟.

Jesus, risen from the dead, ℟.

Jesus, our Lord, ℟.

Jesus, our hope, ℟.

Jesus, our peace, ℟.

Jesus, our Savior, ℟.

Jesus, our salvation, ℟.

Jesus, our Resurrection, ℟.

Jesus, Lord of creation, ℟.

Jesus, lover of all, ℟.

Jesus, life of the world, ℟.

Jesus, freedom for the imprisoned, ℟.

Jesus, joy of the sorrowing, ℟.

Jesus, giver of the Spirit, ℟.

Jesus, giver of good gifts, ℟.

Jesus, source of new life, ℟.

Jesus, Lord of Life, ℟.

Jesus, true Shepherd, ℟.

Prayers of Praise and Thanksgiving 215

Jesus, true Light, ℟.
Jesus, Bread of heaven, ℟.
Jesus, Bread of Life, ℟.
Jesus, Bread of thanksgiving, ℟.
Jesus, life-giving Bread, ℟.
Jesus, holy manna, ℟.
Jesus, new covenant, ℟.
Jesus, food of everlasting life, ℟.
Jesus, food for our journey, ℟.
Jesus, holy banquet, ℟.
Jesus, true sacrifice, ℟.
Jesus, perfect sacrifice, ℟.
Jesus, eternal sacrifice, ℟.
Jesus, divine Victim, ℟.
Jesus, Mediator of the new Covenant, ℟.
Jesus, mystery of the altar, ℟.
Jesus, mystery of faith, ℟.
Jesus, medicine of immortality, ℟.
Jesus, pledge of eternal glory, ℟.

> Jesus, Lamb of God, you take away the sins of the world,
> *have mercy on us.*
> Jesus, Bearer of our sins, you take away the sins
>   of the world,
> *have mercy on us.*

Jesus, Redeemer of the world, you take away
   the sins of the world,
      have mercy on us.

Christ, hear us. *Christ hear us.*
Christ, graciously hear us. *Christ, graciously hear us.*
Lord Jesus, hear our prayer. *Lord Jesus, hear our prayer.*

Prayers of Repentance and Reparation

As disciples of Christ, we are called to live in continual conversion: a demanding spiritual journey in which, recognizing the evil of sin, we daily seek to grow in self-knowledge and in heartfelt contrition for our weakness and sinful choices. Our very discomfort breaks open our hearts to receive the gifts of God's Holy Spirit. Every day we start afresh, trusting always more in God's goodness and mercy, and delighting in God's faithful love.

> The greater my unworthiness, the more abundant God's mercy.
>
> —Saint Elizabeth Ann Seton

> My God, take my heart. Set it on fire!
>
> —Saint Bernadette Soubirous

Act of Contrition

> My God,
> I am sorry for my sins with all my heart.
> In choosing to do wrong
> and failing to do good,

> I have sinned against you
> whom I should love above all things.
> I firmly intend, with your help,
> to do penance,
> to sin no more,
> and to avoid whatever leads me to sin.
> Our Savior Jesus Christ
> suffered and died for us.
> In his name, my God, have mercy.

The Jesus Prayer

> Lord Jesus Christ, Son of David,
> have mercy on me, a sinner.

Psalm 51

> *See page 164.*

Be Merciful

> Be merciful, O Lord, for we have sinned.

Possess Our Hearts

> Lord Jesus, our Savior,
> let us now come to you.
> Our hearts are cold; Lord, warm them with your selfless love.

Our hearts are sinful; Lord, cleanse them with your
   precious Blood.
Our hearts are weak; Lord, strengthen them
   with your joyous spirit.
Our hearts are empty; Lord, fill them with
   your divine presence.
Lord Jesus, our hearts are yours; possess them always
   and only for yourself. Amen.

Saint Augustine

Too Late Have I Loved You

Too late have I loved you, O Beauty so ancient and so new, too late have I loved you! Behold, you were within me, while I was outside: it was there that I sought you, and, a deformed creature, rushed headlong upon these things of beauty that you have made. You were with me, but I was not with you. They kept me far from you, those fair things which, if they were not in you, would not exist at all. You have called to me, and have cried out, and have shattered my deafness. You have blazed forth with light, and have shone upon me, and you have put my blindness to flight! You have sent forth fragrance, and I have drawn in my breath, and I pant after you. I have tasted you, and I hunger and thirst after you. You have touched me, and I have burned for your peace.

Saint Augustine[42]

Litany of Repentance

For the times I have been impatient, ℟. *Lord, have mercy!*
For the times I have been unkind, ℟.
For the times I have acted jealously, ℟.
For my prideful boasting, ℟.
For having acted arrogantly, ℟.
For having acted dishonestly, ℟.
For those times when I have acted selfishly, ℟.
For responding irritably to others, ℟.
For my brooding over past wrongs, ℟.
For the times I rejoiced not in truth, but at injustice, ℟.
For the times when I gave up on others, ℟.
For my lack of faith and hope, ℟.
For setting limits to my love, ℟.

(Include other personal failings if you like.)

Marie Paul Curley, FSP

Repentance and Reunion

> Father, I have sinned against heaven and myself,
> though you created me as your divine work.
> Formed and touched by you,
> my actions should have been divine.
> Because I violated my own human nature,

I have also sinned before you.
Self-inflicted misery is my downfall.
I am no longer worthy of being called your child,
because I have alienated myself
of my own free will
from your creation within me—
the way you have prepared.
Now treat me as your servant,
whose freedom you paid at a high price
in the Blood of your Son.
Through Adam the inheritance of your children
   was lost to me.
But now repentance shall repay the debt of my sins
with the Blood of your Son.

Saint Hildegard of Bingen[43]

To Jesus, Good Shepherd

Jesus, you are the Good Shepherd
who gathers and cares
for the scattered sheep.
The shepherd leads
and the sheep follow
because they recognize the shepherd's voice.
You have given your commandments,
your counsels, your examples.

Whoever heeds them is nourished
with bread that does not perish:
"My food is to do the will of the
heavenly Father."
Have mercy on us when we try to
nourish ourselves
on falsehood or empty pleasures.
Recall us to your way.
Sustain us when we waver, strengthen us when
    we are weak.
May everyone follow you,
Shepherd and Guardian of our souls.
You alone are the Way,
you alone have words of eternal life.
We will follow you wherever you go. Amen.

Adapted from Blessed James Alberione

Litany of the Precious Blood

Lord, have mercy. ℟. *Lord, have mercy.*
Christ, have mercy. ℟. *Christ, have mercy.*
Lord, have mercy. ℟. *Lord, have mercy.*
God our Father in heaven, ℟. *have mercy on us.*
God the Son, Redeemer of the world, ℟.
God the Holy Spirit, ℟.
Holy Trinity, one God, ℟.

Blood of Christ, only-begotten Son
 of the eternal Father, ℟. *save us.*

Blood of Christ, incarnate Word of God, ℟.

Blood of Christ, of the new and eternal covenant, ℟.

Blood of Christ, spilled upon the earth in agony, ℟.

Blood of Christ, shed freely in the scourging, ℟.

Blood of Christ, streaming forth from the crown
 of thorns, ℟.

Blood of Christ, poured out on the Cross, ℟.

Blood of Christ, price of our Redemption, ℟.

Blood of Christ, offering forgiveness and pardon for sin, ℟.

Blood of Christ, Eucharistic refreshment of souls, ℟.

Blood of Christ, river of mercy, ℟.

Blood of Christ, victor over evil, ℟.

Blood of Christ, strength of martyrs, ℟.

Blood of Christ, fortitude of the saints, ℟.

Blood of Christ, sustenance of virgins, ℟.

Blood of Christ, help of those in peril, ℟.

Blood of Christ, relief of the burdened, ℟.

Blood of Christ, solace in sorrow, ℟.

Blood of Christ, hope of the repentant, ℟.

Blood of Christ, consolation of the dying, ℟.

Blood of Christ, peace and comfort for hearts, ℟.

Blood of Christ, pledge of eternal life, ℟.

Blood of Christ, hope of glory, ℟.

Blood of Christ, most worthy of all honor, ℟.

> Lamb of God, you take away the sins of the world,
> *have mercy on us.*
> Lamb of God, you take away the sins of the world,
> *have mercy on us.*
> Lamb of God, you take away the sins of the world,
> *have mercy on us.*
>
> ℣. You redeemed us by your Blood, O Lord.
> ℟. *And made us a kingdom to serve our God.*
>
> *Let us pray.*

Almighty and eternal God, you gave your Son to us to be our Redeemer. Grant that his saving Blood be a safeguard against every evil, so that we may rejoice in its fruits forever in heaven. Through the same Christ our Lord. Amen.

Angel of Fatima's Prayers of Reparation

Most Holy Trinity, Father, Son and Holy Spirit, I adore you profoundly, and I offer you the most precious Body, Blood, soul, and divinity of Jesus Christ, present in all the tabernacles of the world, in reparation for the outrages, sacrileges, and indifference by which he is offended. By the infinite merits of the Sacred Heart of Jesus, and the Immaculate Heart of Mary, I beg of you the conversion of poor sinners.

O my Jesus, forgive us our sins, save us from the fires of hell, lead all souls to heaven, especially those most in need of thy mercy.

My God, I believe, I adore, I trust, and I love thee! I beg pardon for all those that do not believe, do not adore, do not trust, and do not love thee.

Most Holy Trinity, I adore thee! My God, I love thee in the most Blessed Sacrament.

Litany of Reparation to the Most Holy Sacrament

Lord, have mercy on us. ℟. *Christ, have mercy on us.*

Lord, have mercy on us. Christ, hear us. ℟. *Christ, graciously hear us.*

God the Father of heaven, ℟. *have mercy on us.*

God the Son, Redeemer of the world, ℟.

God the Holy Spirit, ℟.

Holy Trinity, one God, ℟.

Sacred Host, offered for the salvation of sinners, ℟.

Sacred Host, humbled at the altar for us and by us, ℟.

Sacred Host, despised and neglected, ℟.

Sacred Host, sign of contradiction, ℟.

Sacred Host, insulted by blasphemers, ℟.

Sacred Host, dishonored by unfaithful ministers, ℟.

Sacred Host, received without love or devotion, ℟.

Sacred Host, forgotten and abandoned in your churches, ℟.

O God, be favorable to us and pardon us. ℟.

O Lord, be favorable to us and hear us. ℟.

For so many unworthy Communions, Lord,
   ℟. *we offer you our reparation.*

For the irreverence of Christians, ℟.

For the unbelief of Catholics, ℟.

For the desecration of your sanctuaries, ℟.

For the holy vessels dishonored and stolen, ℟.

For the blasphemies of the wicked, ℟.

For unworthy conversations carried on in your churches, ℟.

For the sacrileges which profane your Sacrament of love, ℟.

For the indifference of so many of your children, ℟.

For the contempt of your loving invitations, ℟.

For the abuse of your grace, ℟.

For our unfaithfulness and infidelity toward you
   in the most Holy Sacrament, ℟.

For our lukewarmness in loving and serving you, ℟.

For the rejection of those who have left you, ℟.

For your immense sorrow at the loss of souls, ℟.

For an increase in respect towards this adorable
   Mystery in all Christians, ℟. *we beseech you, hear us.*

That you manifest the Sacrament of your love
   to unbelievers, ℟.

Prayers of Repentance and Reparation

That you give us grace to love you in reparation
  for those who hate you, R̷.

That you cast upon us the injuries of those who
  outrage you, R̷.

That you receive our humble reparation, R̷.

That our adoration may be pleasing to you, R̷.

Sacred Host, R̷. *hear us.*

Holy Host, R̷. *graciously hear us.*

> Lamb of God, who takes away the sins of the world,
>   *pardon us.*
> Lamb of God, who takes away the sins of the world,
>   *hear us.*
> Lamb of God, who takes away the sins of the world,
>   *have mercy on us.*

Let us pray.

Lord Jesus Christ, who are pleased to dwell with us in your wonderful Sacrament until the end of time, and by this memory of your passion to render to your Father eternal glory and bestow on us the food of immortality, grant us the grace to mourn with hearts filled with sorrow the many injuries you receive in this adorable Mystery, and the numberless sacrileges committed. Inflame us with an ardent zeal to repair all the insults to which you have preferred to expose yourself, rather than deprive us of your Presence and be separated from us. May we never cease to love and praise you who, with God the Father and the Holy Spirit, live and reign, God, forever and ever. Amen.

Act of Reparation to the Most Blessed Sacrament

> Eucharistic Jesus,
> kneeling before you, I adore you,
> hidden in the most holy Sacrament of the altar,
> and with my whole heart I love you.
> In reparation for all the offences,
> profanations, and sacrileges,
> committed by myself or others against you,
> or that may be committed in times to come,
> I offer to you, my God,
> my humble adoration,
> not indeed as you deserve,
> nor as much as I desire,
> but as far as I am able;
> wishing that I could love you
> with the most perfect love possible.
> I offer you all the discomfort, sorrow, and pain
>   that comes my way
> in reparation for the insults, neglect, and rejection
>   you endure
> in this Sacrament, where you remain for love of us.
> I desire to adore you now and always,

for all those who do not adore or love you.
Yes, my Jesus,
may you be known,
adored, and loved by everyone,
and may thanks be continually given to you
in this most holy Sacrament! Amen.

Mary Leonora Wilson, FSP

Stations of the Cross

You can pray the Way of the Cross following the images in your church, moving from station to station, or, if that is not possible, by simply gazing at a crucifix and calling to mind each individual station. Either way, what is important is to contemplate the great love of Jesus for you and for humanity in undergoing so much suffering and offering his life for our salvation. We suggest that as you accompany Jesus along his sorrowful road to Calvary, you:

Begin each station with the prayer:

We adore you, O Christ, and we bless you,
because by your holy Cross you have redeemed the world.

Call to mind the station with its Scripture prompt and reflect on it.

Offer a brief prayer or aspiration (one is provided for those who wish).

End each station, joining yourself to Mary most holy, with the prayer:

Holy Mother! Pierce me through;
In my heart each wound renew
Of my Savior crucified.

Proceed to the next station.

First Station

Jesus is condemned to death

He was oppressed, and he was afflicted,
> yet he did not open his mouth;
like a lamb that is led to the slaughter (Is 53:7).

Jesus Master, you accept the bitter chalice of death for love of us! You are my example and my strength.

Second Station

Jesus takes up his Cross

We have all turned to our own way,
and the Lord has laid on him
> the iniquity of us all (Is 53:6).

Lord Jesus, I adore your divine love and fortitude. Teach me to respond in love, embracing the Cross when it comes my way.

Third Station

Jesus falls the first time

I am ready to fall,
and my pain is ever with me (Ps 38:17).

Blessed Jesus, even in apparent powerlessness you are redeeming us! Each time I fall may I draw closer to you in trust.

Fourth Station

Jesus meets his afflicted mother

A sword will pierce your soul (see Lk 2:35).

Most Sorrowful Mother, you never abandon your divine Son but remain at his side always. Teach me to love as you love.

Fifth Station

Simon of Cyrene helps Jesus carry the Cross

If any want to become my followers, let them deny
themselves and take up their cross and follow me
(Mk 8:34).

Loving Redeemer, Simon's life was changed by this act of compassion. Accept my offering of love and allow me to lift some of the weight from your rejected Heart.

Sixth Station

Veronica wipes the face of Jesus

I looked for pity, but there was none;
>and for comforters, but I found none (Ps 69:20).

Suffering Jesus, how your face has been disfigured by the tortures you endured! Like Veronica, grant me the grace to recognize your face in everyone I meet.

Seventh Station

Jesus falls the second time

My soul clings to the dust (Ps 119:25).

Lord Jesus Christ, our repeated sins and indifference thrust you to the ground once again. As much as I have offended you, now let me love and adore you even more!

Eighth Station

Jesus comforts the women of Jerusalem

The joy of our hearts has ceased;
>our dancing has been turned to mourning (Lam 5:15).

Merciful Lord, even in your extreme suffering your first thought is for others. Impress the charity of your Heart on my heart!

Ninth Station
Jesus falls the third time

I am utterly spent and crushed (Ps 38:8).

Divine Savior, insults are heaped upon you as you fall again. Let me atone for these by lifting you up in those who are suffering and by offering you adoration and praise.

Tenth Station
Jesus is stripped of his garments

He was despised and rejected by others;
    a man of suffering...
one from whom others hide their faces;
    he was despised, and we held him of no account
        (Is 53:3).

Meek Redeemer, how cruelly you are stripped, and your wounded body exposed! While I weep for those who deride you, let me learn from your forgiveness and compassion.

Eleventh Station
Jesus is nailed to the Cross

They have pierced my hands and my feet;
I can count all my bones.
They stare and gloat over me (see Ps 22:16–17).

Crucified Lord, nailed to the altar of the Cross, slain to ransom us from the grip of Satan! Let my heart never turn away from you again.

Twelfth Station
Jesus dies on the Cross

"Father, into your hands I commend my spirit" (Lk 23:46).

Jesus, Son of God, your sacrifice is complete; you, the Innocent One were immolated to redeem us from our sins. Make my love for you strong and capable of the ultimate sacrifice.

Thirteenth Station
Jesus is taken down from the Cross

Even though I walk through the darkest valley,
> I fear no evil;
for you are with me (Ps 23:4).

Silent Lord, for a brief time death would seem to claim you, but you have conquered death and won eternal life for us. Let me always live for you—now and eternally!

Fourteenth Station
Jesus is laid in the tomb

Weeping may linger for the night,
> but joy comes with the morning (Ps 30:5).

Immortal God, once concealed in the tomb; now concealed under the appearance of bread in our tabernacles. May I keep vigil in adoration before you until I behold your face forever in eternal life.

To Jesus Crucified

Good and gentle Jesus, I kneel before you and with fervent desire ask that you fill my heart with sentiments of faith, hope, and love, repentance for my sins, and true conversion of life.

As I see and contemplate your five precious wounds, I recall the words that David prophesied long ago, my Jesus: "They have pierced my hands and my feet; I can count all my bones" (see Ps 22:17–18).

To conclude the Stations, pray one Our Father, one Hail Mary, and one Glory to the Father for the intentions of the Holy Father.

The Sacrament of Reconciliation

In the sacrament of Reconciliation (also called Penance or confession), we present ourselves contrite before God, who showers his healing grace on our souls. It is a wonderful preparation for receiving Holy Communion. Through this sacrament, God repairs and strengthens our baptismal bonds both with himself and with the Church. Confession brings us to Christ, who fills us with life. Because going to confession can powerfully change us, it's the last thing the devil wants. So we can expect many barriers and obstacles and much emotional resistance to the sacrament. We should go anyway. Jesus wants to meet us in this sacrament and fill us with life so that we may be strengthened against the temptations of Satan and prepared for death and judgment.

While preparing for confession, ask God to help you see and accept the particular sins for which you are responsible. Then explore your behavior since your last confession. One way to jog your mind and heart is through reflection on the Ten Commandments, which helps you focus your thoughts and look over your life.

> After confession, a crown is given to penitents!
> —Saint Alphonsus de Liguori,
> quoting Saint John Chrysostom

Celebrating the Sacrament of Reconciliation

Reflect and understand clearly how your behavior has damaged your relationship with God, the Church, and people in your life.

Begin with a Sign of the Cross and tell the priest how long it has been since your last confession.

Tell the priest your sins.

Listen for any words from him that may help you to deepen your faithfulness to Christ and to avoid repeating the sins.

When the priest gives you a penance, indicate you understand it, or ask for clarification if you don't.

Say an Act of Contrition (see page 217).

Listen to the words of absolution.

Complete your penance.

Thank God for this great moment of grace in your life.

Counsels for Living a Christian Life

The Ten Commandments
See Ex. 20:1–17

I am the Lord your God:
> You shall not have other gods besides me.
>
> You shall not take the name of the Lord your God in vain.
>
> Remember to keep holy the Lord's day.
>
> Honor your father and your mother.

You shall not kill.

You shall not commit adultery.

You shall not steal.

You shall not bear false witness against your neighbor.

You shall not covet your neighbor's wife.

You shall not covet your neighbor's goods.

The Beatitudes

Mt 5:3–12

Blessed are the poor in spirit, for theirs is the kingdom of heaven.

Blessed are those who mourn, for they will be comforted.

Blessed are the meek, for they will inherit the earth.

Blessed are those who hunger and thirst for righteousness, for they will be filled.

Blessed are the merciful, for they will receive mercy.

Blessed are the pure in heart, for they will see God.

Blessed are the peacemakers, for they will be called children of God.

Blessed are those who are persecuted for righteousness' sake, for theirs is the kingdom of heaven.

Blessed are you when people revile you and persecute you and utter all kinds of evil against you falsely on my account. Rejoice and be glad, for your reward is great in heaven, for in the same way they persecuted the prophets who were before you.

Prayers of Intercession and Petition

Asking God for what we need is perhaps the most instinctive prayer we humans can make. God delights when we turn to him in trust, whether our petition is for something great or small. Above all, we pray for the coming of the kingdom of God, for personal transformation in Christ, and for the graces we need to be Christ for others.

True Eucharistic prayer is intercessory: we bring not just ourselves and our own concerns to Jesus in the Eucharist, but also the urgent needs of others from all over the world.

> Be "big-hearted" enough in prayer to embrace everyone in the world.
>
> —Venerable Thecla Merlo, FSP

> When we leave Mass, we ought to go out the way Moses descended Mount Sinai: with his face shining, with his heart brave and strong to face the world's difficulties.
>
> —Saint Oscar Romero[44]

As I Walk in Your Light

Jesus in the Eucharist,
give me the grace of a cheerful heart,
an even temper, sweetness,
gentleness, and brightness of mind
as I walk in your light and by your grace.
I pray you to give me the spirit
of over-abundant, ever-springing love,
which overpowers the vexations of life
by its own riches and strength
and which, above all things, unites me to you
who are the fountain and the center of all mercy, loving kindness, and joy. Amen.

Saint John Henry Newman

God's Dream for Me

Your dream, O Master, is to lay hold of me with your divine life.

Your dream is to purify me, to recreate me, to make me a new person in your image.

Your dream is to fill me with your love, so that I love the Father and all my brothers and sisters just as you do.

Your dream is to draw me to you with the closest bonds, to unite my heart with yours, to make me strong,

to impart to me your divine power so that I can overcome
evil and be constant in doing good.

Your dream is to inflame me with untiring zeal to spread
your kingdom.

Your dream is to possess me in this life and in the life to
come.

May your dream come true! May I be able to give all you
ask of me. Amen.

Adapted from Blessed James Alberione

For Faith in the Real Presence

I come to you, Lord, like the Apostles, to pray, "Increase my faith." Give me a strong and lively faith that you are really present in the Eucharist; an active faith that will direct my life.

Give me the remarkable faith of the centurion, which drew forth such praise from you. Give me the faith of the beloved disciple to recognize you and exclaim, "It is the Lord!" Give me the faith of Peter to confess, "You are the Christ, Son of the living God!" Give me the faith of Mary Magdalen to bow down at your feet and cry out, "Rabboni! Master!"

Give me the faith of all the saints to whom the Eucharist was heaven begun here on earth. Each time I receive the Eucharist and each time I make a visit to the Blessed Sacrament, increase my faith and love, my humility and reverence, and my trust that all good things will come to me.

My Lord and my God, increase my faith!

Prayer for the Gifts of the Holy Spirit

Divine Holy Spirit,
eternal Love of the Father and of the Son,
I adore you, I thank you, I love you,
and I ask your forgiveness
for all the times I have sinned against you
and against my neighbor.
Descend with many graces
on those ordained as bishops and priests,
on those consecrated as men and women religious,
on those who receive the sacrament of Confirmation.
Be light, sanctity, and zeal for them.
To you, Spirit of truth,
I dedicate my mind, imagination, and memory.
Enlighten me.
Bring me to fuller knowledge of Jesus Christ,
and a deeper understanding of the Gospel and
 the teaching of the Church.
Increase in me the gifts of wisdom, knowledge,
 understanding, and counsel.
To you, sanctifying Spirit,
I dedicate my will.
Guide me, make me faithful in living fully
the commandments and my vocation.
Grant me the gifts of fortitude and holy fear of God.
To you, life-giving Spirit,

I dedicate my heart.
Guard me from evil; pour on me an always greater
    abundance of your life.
Bring to completion your work in me.
Grant me the gift of piety. Amen.

Blessed James Alberione

To My Guardian Angel, Companion in Adoration

My Guardian Angel, with your companion angels you constantly behold the face of God. You were created to adore, glorify, and praise the Divine Trinity. Even while helping me in my earthly pilgrimage, you remain always united with God, immersed in his presence and his holiness, beholding his beauty, and radiating his love. Teach me, O blessed companion, to adore the Lord present in the most holy Sacrament of the Eucharist, inspired by your own great love and singleness of heart. Like you, I too have been created to adore, love, and serve God, my Creator and Redeemer. Unlike you, my vision is often obscured by distractions or spiritual darkness. Help me then, dear angel, to pray always, to keep my gaze fixed on Jesus, to walk before the Father with humility, gratitude, and trust. May my life be a living sacrifice of praise and may the fire of adoration always burn lovingly in my heart. With you, I pray:

> "Blessing and glory and wisdom
> and thanksgiving and honor

and power and might
be to our God forever and ever!" (Rev 7:12)

Mary Leonora Wilson, FSP

Act of Trust in the Divine Master

The Master is here and is calling you (see Jn 11:28).

The Master is here in my personal story with its lights and shadows. Jesus is calling me to accept my story as he does and to explore the vast horizons of his peace.

The Master is here in my work and in my service.

The Master is here in my family and my community. He is calling me to communicate with them, to trust and to live his love.

The Master is here in the Church, in its efforts for evangelization and service, in the liturgy, which pulsates with the power of the Holy Spirit. Jesus is calling me to contemplate his mysteries as they unfold throughout the liturgical year.

The Master is here in the poor and the oppressed, in those who suffer or have lost their way, in those who need the light of my faith and the gift of my love.

The Master is here in the depths of my heart. He is calling me to open the door to him so that he might dwell within me, his chosen home.

Giovannamaria Carrara, FSP

Heart of Love

O Heart of love,
I place my trust entirely in you.
Though I fear all things from my weakness,
I hope all things from your goodness!

Saint Margaret Mary Alacoque

Prayer of Saint Francis

Lord, make me an instrument of your peace:
where there is hatred, let me sow love;
where there is discord, harmony;
where there is injury, pardon;
where there is error, truth;
where there is doubt, faith;
where there is despair, hope;
where there is darkness, light;
where there is sadness, joy.

Divine Master, grant that I may not so much seek
to be consoled as to console;
to be understood, as to understand;
to be loved, as to love.
For it is in giving that we receive;
it is in forgetting self that we find ourselves;
it is in pardoning that we are pardoned;
and it is in dying that we are born to eternal life.

Prayer of Surrender

Father, I abandon myself into your hands;
do with me what you will.
Whatever you may do, I thank you;
I am ready for all, I accept all.
Let only your will be done in me,
and in all your creatures.
I wish no more than this, O Lord.
Into your hands I commend myself;
I offer myself to you with all the love of my heart,
for I love you, Lord, and so need to give myself,
to surrender myself into your hands without reserve,
and with boundless confidence, for you are my Father.

Saint Charles de Foucauld

Shine Through Me

Dear Jesus, help me to spread your fragrance everywhere I go. Flood my soul with your Spirit and life. Penetrate and possess my whole being so utterly that my life may only be a radiance of yours.

Shine through me and be so in me that every person I come in contact with may feel your presence in my soul. Let them look up, and see no longer me, but only Jesus! Stay with me and then I shall begin to shine as you shine, shining so as to be a light to others. The light, Jesus, will be all from you; none of it will be mine. It will be you shining on others through me. Let me thus praise you in the way that you love best, by shining on those around me.

Let me preach you without preaching, not by my words but by my example, by the catching force, the sympathetic influence of what I do, the evident fullness of the love my heart bears for you. Amen.

Saint John Henry Newman

Soul of Jesus

Soul of Jesus, sanctify me.
Blood of Jesus, wash me.
Passion of Jesus, comfort me.
Wounds of Jesus, hide me.
Heart of Jesus, receive me.
Spirit of Jesus, enliven me.
Goodness of Jesus, pardon me.
Beauty of Jesus, draw me.
Humility of Jesus, humble me.
Peace of Jesus, pacify me.
Love of Jesus, inflame me.
Kingdom of Jesus, come to me.
Grace of Jesus, replenish me.
Mercy of Jesus, pity me.
Sanctity of Jesus, sanctify me.
Purity of Jesus, purify me.

Cross of Jesus, support me.
Nails of Jesus, hold me.
Mouth of Jesus, bless me in life, defend me in the hour of death.
Mouth of Jesus, call me to come to you
and receive me with your saints in glory evermore.

Let us pray.

Unite me to you, O adorable Jesus. Life-giving heavenly Bread, feed me, sanctify me, reign in me, transform me into yourself; live in me and let me live in you; let me adore you in your life-giving Sacrament as my God, listen to you as to my Master, obey you as my King, imitate you as my Model, follow you as my Shepherd, love you as my Father, seek you as my Physician who heals all the maladies of my soul. Be indeed my Way, Truth, and Life; sustain me, O heavenly Manna, through the desert of this world, till I shall behold you unveiled in glory. Amen.

Saint Elizabeth Ann Seton

Come, Holy Spirit

Come, Holy Spirit, fill the hearts of your faithful
and enkindle in them the fire of your love.
Send forth your Spirit and they shall be created,
and you shall renew the face of the earth.

For Protection and Enlightenment

> May the strength of God pilot us.
> May the power of God preserve us.
> May the wisdom of God instruct us.
> May the hand of God protect us.
> May the way of God direct us.
> May the shield of God defend us.
> May the hosts of God protect us.
> Now and always.

Saint Patrick

Prayer for the Needs of Others

> God of love, whose compassion never fails,
> we bring you the sufferings of the world,
> the needs of the homeless,
> the cries of prisoners,
> the pains of the sick and injured,
> the sorrow of the bereaved,
> the helplessness of the elderly and weak.
> According to their needs and your great mercy,
> strengthen and relieve them
> in Jesus Christ our Lord.

Saint Anselm

In Our Daily Living

Lord of the world and of peace,
help us to unite these two words
in our daily life.
Peace in the world and peace in our hearts—
this we ask of you, Lord,
for if there is to be peace in the world,
there must be peace in our hearts.
Remove from us hate and rancor
and everything that impedes
a serene and happy way of life.
Give us your peace, O Lord,
the peace that the world often
does not understand or value,
but without which,
the world cannot live.

Gloria Bordeghini, FSP

Prayer for Priests

Jesus, eternal High Priest,
bless all priests so that they may fulfill their priestly
    vocation:
to believe profoundly,
to profess their faith with courage,
to pray fervently,

to teach with deep conviction,
to serve,
to put into practice in their own lives
the program of the beatitudes,
to know how to love disinterestedly,
to be close to everyone,
especially those who are most in need.

Adapted from Saint John Paul II[45]

To Foster Respect for Life

O Mary, bright dawn of the new world,
Mother of the living, to you do we entrust the cause
  of life:
Look down, O Mother, upon the vast numbers
of babies not allowed to be born,
of the poor whose lives are made difficult,
of men and women who are victims of brutal violence,
of the elderly and the sick killed by indifference or
  out of misguided mercy.
Grant that all who believe in your Son
may proclaim the Gospel of life with honesty and love
to the people of our time.
Obtain for them the grace to accept that Gospel as
  a gift ever new,
the joy of celebrating it with gratitude throughout
  their lives,

and the courage to bear witness to it resolutely,
in order to build, together with all people of goodwill,
the civilization of truth and love,
to the praise and glory of God,
the Creator and lover of life.

Saint John Paul II[46]

Prayer of Saint Gertrude for the Souls in Purgatory

Eternal Father, in union with the Masses said throughout the world today, I offer you the most precious Blood of your divine Son, Jesus, for all the holy souls in purgatory, for sinners everywhere, for sinners in the universal Church, for those in my own home and within my family. Amen.

Saint Gertrude

Divine Mercy Chaplet

*The Divine Mercy Chaplet is prayed on an ordinary five-decade rosary.
Begin with an Our Father, Hail Mary, and Apostles' Creed.
On the single bead before each decade:*

Eternal Father, I offer you the Body and Blood, soul and divinity of your dearly beloved Son, our Lord Jesus Christ, in atonement for our sins and those of the whole world.

On the ten beads of each decade:

For the sake of his sorrowful passion, have mercy on us and on the whole world.

After the five decades, conclude with:

Holy God, Holy Mighty One, Holy Immortal One, have mercy on us and on the whole world (*three times*).

Saint Faustina Kowalska

Invocations to the Eucharistic Heart of Jesus

In the following invocations, we confidently remind Jesus of the Promises of his own Sacred Heart made to Saint Margaret Mary Alacoque.

Eucharistic Heart of Jesus, grant peace to our families: *We trust in your promise.*

Eucharistic Heart of Jesus, grant us all the graces necessary for our state of life: *We trust in your promise.*

Eucharistic Heart of Jesus, console us in our suffering: *We trust in your promise.*

Eucharistic Heart of Jesus, be our safe shelter in each troubled hour of our life: *We trust in your promise.*

Eucharistic Heart of Jesus, be our refuge in the moment of death: *We trust in your promise.*

Eucharistic Heart of Jesus, abundantly bless all our undertakings: *We trust in your promise.*

Eucharistic Heart of Jesus, be the source and ocean of mercy for all of us sinners: *We trust in your promise.*

Eucharistic Heart of Jesus, change the lukewarm into your fervent lovers: *We trust in your promise.*

Eucharistic Heart of Jesus, let the fervent rise quickly to great perfection: *We trust in your promise.*

Eucharistic Heart of Jesus, bless the places and houses where your image is displayed and honored: *We trust in your promise.*

Eucharistic Heart of Jesus, give priests the power to move the most hardened hearts: *We trust in your promise.*

Eucharistic Heart of Jesus, write on your Heart the names of those who spread your devotion: *We trust in your promise.*

Eucharistic Heart of Jesus, grant the grace of everlasting life to those who, for nine months and with sentiments of reparation, receive Communion on the First Friday: *We trust in your promise.*

Eucharistic Heart of Jesus, refresh all those who come to you oppressed and weary: *We trust in your promise.*

Eucharistic Heart of Jesus, grant us all the graces that we ask of the Father in your name: *We trust in your promise.*

Eucharistic Heart of Jesus, send good workers into your harvest: *We trust in your promise.*

Eucharistic Heart of Jesus, grant goodwill to all who ask it of you: *We trust in your promise.*

Eucharistic Heart of Jesus, grant us the gift of wisdom: *We trust in your promise.*

Eucharistic Heart of Jesus, grant the Church perpetual triumph over hell: *We trust in your promise.*

Eucharistic Heart of Jesus, give the living water of holiness to whoever asks for it: *We trust in your promise.*

Eucharistic Heart of Jesus, remain always with your apostles of the word and the pen: *We trust in your promise.*

Eucharistic Heart of Jesus, be with the family that prays together: *We trust in your promise.*

Eucharistic Heart of Jesus, always hear our prayers in life and in death: *We trust in your promise.*

Let us pray.

Father, in the death and Resurrection of your Son you redeemed all people. Guard your work of mercy in us so that, in assiduous celebration of the paschal mystery, we will receive the fruits of our salvation. Through Christ our Lord. Amen.

Blessed James Alberione

In Adoration with Mary

Many saints eloquently encourage us to follow their example of making Mary our way to Jesus. Saint Peter Julian Eymard puts it well:

> Where shall we find Jesus on earth if not in Mary's arms? Did she not give us the Eucharist? Was it not her consent to the Incarnation of the Word in her pure womb that inaugurated the great mystery of reparation to God and union with us, which Jesus accomplished by his mortal life, and that he continues in the Eucharist?
>
> Without Mary, we shall not find Jesus, for she possesses him in her Heart. There he takes his delight, and those who wish to know his inmost virtues, his sacred and privileged love, must seek them in the Heart of Mary. Those who love that good Mother will find Jesus in her pure Heart.
>
> We must never separate Jesus from Mary. We can go to him only through her.[47]

Three compelling reasons for going to Jesus through Mary are:

1. From the Cross, Jesus gave us Mary as our Mother;

2. God chose Mary to be his own Mother;

3. Mary was the first adorer of her Son and his first and closest disciple.

In praying to Mary, we entrust ourselves to her motherly care, as Jesus invites us. "Behold your mother!" (see Jn 19:27)

> Look up at the star, call on Mary! With her for a guide, you will never go astray.
>
> — Saint Bernard of Clairvaux

> Like a branch ever bearing its fruit and offering it to everyone, Mary always gives Jesus: suffering, glorious, Eucharistic, the Way, Truth, and Life of humanity.
>
> —Blessed James Alberione

The Mysteries of the Rosary: Eucharistic Reflections

The Joyful Mysteries

Usually prayed on Mondays and Saturdays

In these Joyful Mysteries, we meditate on the reality of Jesus Christ's presence among us in the Holy Eucharist. Each mystery has a Eucharistic reflection and the option of praying for the grace to imitate a particular Eucharistic virtue.

1. The Annunciation to the Blessed Virgin Mary (Lk 1:26–38)

The archangel Gabriel announces to Mary the coming of the Savior and Mary's divine motherhood. At her assent, the Son of God "empties himself" of the trappings of divinity and is conceived by the Virgin Mary, who lovingly receives him and adores him as his handmaid. Mary becomes the first tabernacle of the Word made flesh, his first and most perfect adorer.

Eucharistic virtue: Humility

2. Mary Visits Her Cousin Elizabeth (Lk 1:39–45)

In Mary's visit, Saint Elizabeth recognizes the presence of her Lord: "How is it that the mother of my Lord should come to *me*?" (see Lk 1:43). In the Holy Eucharist, Jesus is really, truly present in our midst, even though hidden under ordinary appearances. Joyful recognition, thanksgiving, and praise are the most appropriate responses we can give at every Eucharistic encounter.

When we receive the Lord as Mary did, we become *living* tabernacles, who bring Jesus to others wherever we go.

Eucharistic virtue: Love for one's neighbor

3. The Birth of Jesus at Bethlehem (Lk 2:1–7)

The Incarnation and the Eucharist, two of the greatest mysteries of our faith, are astonishing expressions of God's love for us. Out of love for us, our humble God becomes a baby, drawing unimaginably close to us, making himself vulnerable to sinful human beings. Hiding his divinity so that he can be in our midst seems to us to be beneath his divine dignity, but not to God! How lovable as a tiny Infant! And how infinitely lovable even more in his humble presence in the Eucharist!

Eucharistic virtue: Poverty of spirit

4. The Presentation of Jesus in the Temple (Lk 2:22–24)

Mary and Joseph present Jesus in the Temple, fulfilling the Law and offering him back to the Father. Mary and Joseph were not only consecrating Jesus to fulfill his divine mission but were saying a wholehearted "yes" to participating in that mission—a participation in which Mary would sacrifice her Heart as Jesus would sacrifice his life.

Like Mary, we too are called to participate in Jesus' sacrifice on the Cross, an oblation that Jesus renews in every Eucharist. With him, we offer ourselves to the Father in all our joys and sufferings.

Eucharistic virtue: Spirit of loving sacrifice

5. The Finding of the Child Jesus in the Temple (Lk 2:41–51)

After three frantic days of searching, Mary and Joseph find twelve-year-old Jesus teaching in the Temple. Jesus is found... but he was never truly lost: "I must be in my Father's house." Mary and Joseph surely felt that *they* were the ones who were lost during those three dark days as they sought Jesus with anguished longing. When we feel like we have lost Jesus or are longing for the peace, joy, and fulfillment that only God can give, let us go to the tabernacle! We will always *be found* in his Eucharistic presence.

Eucharistic virtue: Longing for the Bread of Life

THE LUMINOUS MYSTERIES

Usually prayed on Thursdays

In these Luminous Mysteries, we meditate on the reality of Jesus Christ's saving work among us and for us.

1. John Baptizes Jesus in the Jordan (Mt 3:13–17)

When John the Baptist baptizes Jesus, the Father affirms Jesus' identity as his Beloved Son. In his life, death, and Resurrection, Jesus won for us the privilege of becoming God's cherished sons and daughters, an identity we received at our Baptism that can never be taken away. Every time we encounter Jesus in the Eucharist, Jesus affirms, nurtures, and deepens our identity as God's beloved ones.

Eucharistic virtue: Gratitude for our identity as beloved in Christ

2. Jesus Reveals His Glory at the Wedding of Cana (Jn 2:1–11)

At Mary's request, Jesus turns water into wine, providing an abundance of wine for the wedding feast. This miracle, containing so many Eucharistic allusions, comes about because Mary so confidently trusts in her Son's saving mission.

Mary's request to Jesus launches his public ministry and helps the disciples to begin to see who Jesus truly is. Mary always leads us to Jesus; she encourages us to open our hearts to faith in his saving work in our lives: "Do whatever he tells you" (Jn. 2:5). She is the one who can best help us to live a truly Eucharistic life.

Eucharistic virtue: Confident trust in Jesus

3. Jesus Proclaims the Kingdom of God and Calls Us to Conversion (Mk 1:14–15)

Jesus invites all to enter the kingdom of God with the words, "Repent, and believe in the good news" (Mk. 1:15). We begin every Mass expressing our sorrow for our sins. Frequently receiving the Sacrament of Penance delights the Lord and removes any obstacles to Jesus bringing about the kingdom of God more fully in us when we receive him in Holy Communion. No one is ever truly worthy to receive our Eucharistic Lord, but we *can* prepare our hearts to be a place of joy and consolation for him.

Eucharistic virtue: Spirit of repentance and reparation

4. The Transfiguration of Jesus (Lk 9:28–36)

On Mount Tabor when Jesus is transfigured before the three apostles, they wanted to remain and bask in the radiance of his glory. This glorious moment of light was meant to strengthen the apostles during Christ's upcoming passion and death. In the presence of the hidden glory of the Eucharistic Jesus, as we bask in the light of his tender and victorious love, we can ask Jesus for the gift to unite our moments of darkness and pain with his self-offering to the Father.

Eucharistic virtue: Fortitude

5. Jesus Gives Us the Eucharist (Jn 6:22–65)

On the night he was betrayed, Jesus gave us the unsurpassable gift of his very self in the Holy Eucharist, to make present to us for all time the sacrifice of the Cross that he offered to the Father for our salvation on Calvary: "Before the festival of the Passover, Jesus knew that his hour had come to depart from this world and go to the Father. Having loved his own who were in the world, he loved them to the end" (Jn. 13:1).

Jesus gives himself to us in love in the Holy Eucharist to enable us to live his last request, "Abide in my love" (Jn 15:9).

Eucharistic virtue: Union with Christ

The Sorrowful Mysteries

Usually prayed on Tuesdays and Fridays

In the Sorrowful Mysteries, we meditate on the tremendous love of the Lord for us and the urgency for us to respond to him in love and reparation. An option to offer reparatory intentions with each decade is suggested.

1. Jesus Prays in the Garden of Gethsemane (Lk 22:39–46)

Jesus is overcome with anguish and dread over the sufferings he is about to face: especially the devastating weight of the sins of all humanity, which he is taking on himself. He first turns to the Father in prayer but then seeks out his chosen apostles, who, instead of waiting up with him, abandon him by falling asleep. "Could you not watch one hour with me?" was his desolate cry in the Garden of Gethsemane, but how many times has Jesus repeated it from the tabernacles in the empty churches where he is always available?

Reparatory intention: In reparation for the times when Jesus in the Holy Eucharist has been ignored, neglected, or abandoned.

2. Jesus Is Scourged at the Pillar (Jn 19:1)

After his arrest and mock trial, the most sacred Body of Christ, from whom so many had found healing, is most cruelly scourged. His sacred Blood freely soaks into the ground. Yet the Son of God humbly submits to this heinous torture. How can we give greater reverence and adoration to Christ's same sacred Body and Blood present on every altar, in every tabernacle?

Reparatory intention: In reparation for the sacrileges, blasphemies, or other acts of disrespect committed against Jesus in the most Blessed Sacrament.

3. Jesus Is Crowned with Thorns (Mk 15:16–20)

The Word of Life, the One who *is* Truth, is ridiculed and mocked as a false king and crowned with thorns. Jesus remains silent against this gratuitous brutality. He remains defenseless like all the poor ones of this world who have no protection against misunderstanding, derision, or savagely callous abuse. Jesus' Eucharistic littleness reminds us how precious the "little ones" of the world are to him.

Reparatory intention: In reparation for those who mock the Eucharist and the love of Christ, for those who mock Christ present in others, and for those who have rejected the gift of faith that they have received.

4. Jesus Carries the Cross to Calvary (Jn 19:17)

Jesus takes the cross upon his shoulders, but as heavy as the wood of the Cross was, heavier by far to bear is the evil of the sins of all humanity. Each excruciating step Jesus takes must have felt beyond his strength, but he keeps going. Every step of Jesus' way of the Cross is an act of unprecedented love and fidelity for the Father and for you: a faithful love you behold every time you encounter him in the Eucharist, and a faithful love that he calls you to imitate.

Reparatory intention: In reparation for those who, out of weakness or human respect, make poor Communions, receive Jesus while in the state of grievous sin, or miss going to Mass on Sundays.

5. Jesus Dies for Our Sins (Jn 19:30)

At every Mass, Jesus offers himself in that same sacrifice to the Father on our behalf. The Eucharist is a mystery of love beyond words, beyond our comprehension. Jesus explains what he wants us to understand and live by his passion and death: "No one has greater love than this, to lay down one's life for one's friends. You are my friends if you do what I command you" (Jn 15:13–14).

Reparatory intention: In reparation for our own sins, the sins of family and friends, and the sins of those souls who are called to a greater life of love, especially devout laity, bishops and priests, religious brothers and sisters.

The Glorious Mysteries

Usually prayed on Wednesdays and Sundays

In the Glorious Mysteries of the Rosary, we contemplate with gratitude and awe the Eucharistic face of the Risen Christ who victoriously leads us past all obstacles of this earthly life to share in his life for a glorious eternity, a life of which the Eucharistic banquet is a pledge and foretaste. Every decade also includes a suggested intention of gratitude for the mystery of the Eucharist.

1. Jesus Rises from the Dead (Jn 20:1–10)

The Eucharistic Host that we receive and adore is the glorious Body, Blood, soul, and divinity of the Risen Christ: the very Christ before whose majesty angels tremble and whose wounds pulse with love for us, and who has promised us, "I am the living bread that came down from heaven. Whoever eats of this bread will live forever; and the bread that I will give for the life of the world is my flesh" (Jn 6:51).

In thanksgiving: for the gift of every Holy Communion, and the nourishment, strength, and life Jesus gives us in the Eucharist.

2. Jesus Ascends into Heaven (Mk 16:19–20)

Before ascending into heaven, Jesus promises, "Behold, I am with you all days, even to the consummation of the world."

Jesus fulfills this promise in many ways in the Church, but the most striking is his astonishing gift of himself in the Eucharist at every Mass and his continual presence in the tabernacle!

In thanksgiving: for the gift of Jesus' Real Presence in the Eucharist and his constant availability in tabernacles throughout the world.

3. The Holy Spirit Descends on the Apostles (Ac 2:1–4)

The Acts of the Apostles tells us that Mary accompanies the apostles in prayer in the Upper Room, helping them prepare to receive the power and gifts of the Holy Spirit. We ask Mary, woman of the Eucharist and spouse of the Spirit, to help us cultivate greater receptivity to the Holy Spirit, who will set our hearts aflame so that we can fulfill Jesus' command at the Last Supper: "Love one another as I have loved you" (Jn 15:12).

In thanksgiving: for the transforming gifts of the Holy Spirit poured out at every Mass and in every Communion, enabling us to live a truly Eucharistic life of love and service.

4. Mary Is Assumed, Body and Soul, into Heaven (Lk 1:48–49)

By taking on our humanity, Jesus blesses our human bodies with a special promise of heavenly glory, and he promises even more to those who receive the Bread of Life: "This is the bread that came down from heaven, not like that which your ancestors ate, and they died. But the one who eats this bread will live forever" (Jn. 6:58). Jesus anticipates this promise for his Mother in her Assumption, and thus reassures us that we, too, will be raised up on the last day.

In thanksgiving: for the promise of eternal life that the Eucharistic Jesus gives us.

5. Mary Is Crowned Queen of Heaven and Earth (2 Tm 2:12)

The Eucharist Banquet, a preview of the heavenly banquet, is our "pledge of future glory" and a foretaste of the salvation Jesus won for us in his paschal mystery. We could also say that Jesus' Eucharistic love for us is also a pledge and foretaste of the embrace of divine love that is heaven.

In thanksgiving: for the salvation Jesus won for us and makes sacramentally present at every Eucharist.

Eucharistic Mysteries of the Rosary

These Eucharistic mysteries, intended to be prayed as we do the traditional mysteries of the Rosary, are offered here as a help to contemplate one of the greatest mysteries of our faith: the Holy Eucharist.

1. Jesus Multiplies the Loaves and Fishes (Mk 6:30–44)

The hour is late. Jesus has been teaching the enormous crowd of people all day, breaking open for them the bread of God's word. His disciples approach Jesus with a request that precipitates this miracle foreshadowing the Eucharist:

> When it grew late, his disciples came to him and said, "This is a deserted place, and the hour is now very late; send them away so that they may go into the surrounding country and villages and buy something for themselves to eat." But he answered them, "You give them something to eat." They said to him, "Are we to go and buy two hundred denarii worth of bread, and give it to them to eat?" And he said to them, "How many loaves have you? Go and see." When they had found out, they said, "Five, and two fish." Taking the five loaves and the two fish, he looked up to heaven, and blessed and broke the loaves, and gave them to his disciples to set before the people; and he divided the two fish among them all. And all ate and were filled; and they took up twelve baskets full of broken pieces and of the fish. Those who had eaten the loaves numbered five thousand men. (Mk 6: 35–38, 41–44)

2. Jesus Gives the Bread of Life Discourse (Jn 6:22–71)

Having been filled with the miraculous loaves, the people want more. But are they ready for the fullness of life that Jesus wants to give them? Are we?

> "Very truly, I tell you, whoever believes has eternal life. I am the bread of life. Your ancestors ate the manna in the wilderness, and they died. This is the bread that comes down from heaven, so that one may eat of it and not die. I am the living bread that came down from heaven. Whoever eats of this bread will live forever; and the bread that I will give for the life of the world is my flesh."
>
> The Jews then disputed among themselves, saying, "How can this man give us his flesh to eat?" So Jesus said to them, "Very truly, I tell you, unless you eat the flesh of the Son of Man and drink his blood, you have no life in you. Those who eat my flesh and drink my blood have eternal life, and I will raise them up on the last day; for my flesh is true food and my blood is true drink. Those who eat my flesh and drink my blood abide in me, and I in them." (Jn 6: 47–56)

3. Jesus Institutes the Holy Eucharist (Lk 22:17–38)

Jesus' passion is about to begin, that great act of redemption carried out for love of us, but Jesus longs to do even more: he desires to perpetuate his redeeming act of love through his sacramental presence among us.

> When the hour came, he took his place at the table, and the apostles with him. He said to them, "I have eagerly desired to

eat this Passover with you before I suffer; for I tell you, I will not eat it until it is fulfilled in the kingdom of God." Then he took a cup, and after giving thanks he said, "Take this and divide it among yourselves; for I tell you that from now on I will not drink of the fruit of the vine until the kingdom of God comes." Then he took a loaf of bread, and when he had given thanks, he broke it and gave it to them, saying, "This is my body, which is given for you. Do this in remembrance of me." And he did the same with the cup after supper, saying, "This cup that is poured out for you is the new covenant in my blood." (Lk 22:14–20)

4. Jesus Sacrifices His Life for Us on Calvary (Jn 19:16–30)

The "Hour" has come: Jesus gives himself up for us, offering his life on the altar of the Cross to save us. This sacrifice is the great memorial of his love.

So they took Jesus; and carrying the cross by himself, he went out to what is called The Place of the Skull, which in Hebrew is called Golgotha. There they crucified him. . . .

Standing near the cross of Jesus were his mother, and his mother's sister, Mary the wife of Clopas, and Mary Magdalene. When Jesus saw his mother and the disciple whom he loved standing beside her, he said to his mother, "Woman, here is your son." Then he said to the disciple, "Here is your mother." And from that hour the disciple took her into his own home.

After this, when Jesus knew that all was now finished, he said (in order to fulfill the scripture), "I am thirsty." A jar full of sour wine was standing there. So they put a sponge full of the wine on a branch of hyssop and held it to his mouth. When

Jesus had received the wine, he said, "It is finished." Then he bowed his head and gave up his spirit. (Jn 19:16–18, 25–30)

5. Jesus Appears to the Disciples on the Way to Emmaus (Lk 24:13–35)

It's the third day after the Crucifixion, but the truth of the Resurrection has not yet hit home for the disciples. Unrecognized, Jesus catches up with two discouraged disciples as they leave Jerusalem, revealing himself only at the end in the "breaking of bread."

> Beginning with Moses and all the prophets, he [Jesus] interpreted to them the things about himself in all the scriptures. As they came near the village to which they were going, he walked ahead as if he were going on. But they urged him strongly, saying, "Stay with us, because it is almost evening and the day is now nearly over." So he went in to stay with them. When he was at the table with them, he took bread, blessed and broke it, and gave it to them. Then their eyes were opened, and they recognized him; and he vanished from their sight. They said to each other, "Were not our hearts burning within us while he was talking to us on the road, while he was opening the scriptures to us?" That same hour they got up and returned to Jerusalem; and they found the eleven and their companions gathered together. They were saying, "The Lord has risen indeed, and he has appeared to Simon!" Then they told what had happened on the road, and how he had been made known to them in the breaking of the bread. (Lk 24:27–35)

Litany of Loreto

Lord, have mercy on us. ℟. *Christ, have mercy on us.*

Lord, have mercy on us. Christ, hear us.

   ℟. *Christ, graciously hear us.*

God the Father of heaven, ℟. *have mercy on us.*

God the Son, Redeemer of the world, ℟.

God the Holy Spirit, ℟.

Holy Trinity, one God, ℟.

Holy Mary, ℟. *pray for us.*

Holy Mother of God, ℟.

Holy Virgin of virgins, ℟.

Mother of Christ, ℟.

Mother of the Church, ℟.

Mother of mercy, ℟.

Mother of divine grace, ℟.

Mother of hope, ℟.

Mother most pure, ℟.

Mother most chaste, ℟.

Mother inviolate, ℟.

Mother undefiled, ℟.

Mother most amiable, ℟.

Mother most admirable, ℟.

Mother of good counsel, ℟.

Mother of our Creator, ℟.

Mother of our Redeemer, ℟.

Virgin most prudent, ℟.

Virgin most venerable, ℟.

Virgin most renowned, ℟.

Virgin most powerful, ℟.

Virgin most merciful, ℟.

Virgin most faithful, ℟.

Mirror of justice, ℟.

Seat of wisdom, ℟.

Cause of our joy, ℟.

Spiritual vessel, ℟.

Vessel of honor, ℟.

Singular vessel of devotion, ℟.

Mystical rose, ℟.

Tower of David, ℟.

Tower of ivory, ℟.

House of gold, ℟.

Ark of the covenant, ℟.

Gate of heaven, ℟.

Morning star, ℟.

Health of the sick, ℟.

Refuge of sinners, ℟.

Solace of migrants, ℟.

Comforter of the afflicted, ℟.

Help of Christians, ℟.

Queen of angels, ℟.

Queen of patriarchs, ℟.

Queen of prophets, ℟.

Queen of apostles, ℟.

Queen of martyrs, ℟.

Queen of confessors, ℟.

Queen of virgins, ℟.

Queen of all saints, ℟.

Queen conceived without original sin, ℟.

Queen assumed into heaven, ℟.

Queen of the holy Rosary, ℟.

Queen of families, ℟.

Queen of peace, ℟.

>Lamb of God, who takes away the sins of the world, *spare us, O Lord.*
>Lamb of God, who takes away the sins of the world, *graciously spare us, O Lord.*
>Lamb of God, who takes away the sins of the world, *have mercy on us.*

℣. Pray for us, O holy Mother of God,
℟. That we may be made worthy of the promises of Christ.

Let us pray.

Grant, we beseech you, O Lord God, that we your servants may enjoy lasting health of mind and body, and by the glorious intercession of the Blessed Mary, ever Virgin, be delivered from present sorrow and enter into the joy of eternal happiness. Through Christ our Lord. Amen.

Our Lady of the Most Blessed Sacrament

Our Lady of the most Blessed Sacrament, Mother and Model of Adorers, pray for us who have recourse to you.

Saint Peter Julian Eymard

The Angelus

℣. The angel of the Lord declared unto Mary.
℟. And she conceived of the Holy Spirit.
Hail Mary . . .

℣. Behold the handmaid of the Lord.
℟. Be it done unto me according to thy word.
Hail Mary . . .

℣. And the Word was made flesh.
℟. And dwelt among us.
Hail Mary . . .

℣. Pray for us, O holy Mother of God,
℟. That we may be made worthy of the promises of Christ.

Let us pray.

Pour forth, we beseech thee, O Lord, thy grace into our hearts; that we, to whom the Incarnation of Christ, thy Son, was made known by the message of an angel, may by his passion and Cross be brought to the glory of his Resurrection. Through the same Christ, our Lord. Amen.

Glory be to the Father . . .

Memorare

> Remember, O most gracious Virgin Mary,
> that never was it known
> that anyone who fled to your protection,
> implored your help, or sought your intercession
> was left unaided.
> Inspired with this confidence, I fly to you,
> O Virgin of virgins, my Mother.
> To you I come, before you I stand, sinful and sorrowful.
> O Mother of the Word Incarnate, despise not
>   my petitions,
> but in your mercy hear and answer me. Amen.

We Fly to Your Protection

We fly to your protection,
O holy Mother of God;
Despise not our petitions in our necessities,
but deliver us always from all dangers,
O glorious and blessed Virgin. Amen.

Oldest known prayer to the Virgin

Hail, Holy Queen

Hail, holy Queen, Mother of mercy, our life, our sweetness, and our hope! To you we cry, poor banished children of Eve; to you we send up our sighs, mourning and weeping in this valley of tears. Turn then, most gracious advocate, your eyes of mercy toward us, and after this our exile, show unto us the blessed fruit of your womb, Jesus. O clement, O loving, O sweet Virgin Mary.

Magnificat

See page 178.

O Mary, My Queen

O Mary, my Queen, I cast myself into the arms of your mercy.

I place my soul and body under your blessed care and your special protection.

I entrust to you all my hopes and consolations, all my anxieties and sufferings, my entire life, and the final hours of my life.

Through your most holy intercession, grant that all of my works may be directed and carried out according to your will and the will of your divine Son. Amen.

Saint Louis de Montfort

Act of Consecration

Receive me, O Mary, Mother, Teacher, and Queen, among those whom you love, nourish, sanctify, and guide, in the school of Jesus Christ, the Divine Master.

You see in the mind of God those whom he calls, and for them you have special prayers, grace, light, and consolations. My Master, Jesus Christ, entrusted himself wholly to you from the Incarnation to the Ascension. For me this is doctrine, example, and an ineffable gift. I too place myself entirely into your hands. Obtain for me the grace to know, imitate, and love ever more the Divine Master, Way, Truth, and Life. Present me to Jesus, for I am an unworthy sinner, and I have no other recommendation to be admitted to his school than your recommendation. Enlighten my mind, fortify my will, sanctify my heart during this year of my spiritual work, so that I may profit from this great mercy, and may say at the end: "I live now not I, but Christ lives in me."

Blessed James Alberione

Prayer to the Mother of All Adorers

O Mary, teach us the life of adoration!
Teach us to see, as you did, all the mysteries and
    all the graces in the Eucharist;
to live over again the Gospel story and to read it
in the light of the Eucharistic life of Jesus.
Remember, our Lady of the most Blessed Sacrament,
that you are the Mother of all adorers of the
    Holy Eucharist.

Saint Peter Julian Eymard

Hail Mary, of Whom Was Born Our Eucharistic Jesus

Hail Mary, of whom was born our Eucharistic Jesus!

Blessed are you among women, O Mary, and blessed is our Eucharistic Jesus, the fruit of your womb!

O Mary, fruitful vine that has given us the Eucharistic Wine, be forever blessed!

Hail Mary, vessel of purest gold, containing sweetness itself, our Eucharistic Jesus, the Manna of our souls!

O Mary, you are the true mystical table upon which we find the delicious food for our souls, Jesus in the Eucharist.

O Heart of Mary, magnificent throne of the hidden God, be exalted to the heights of the heavens!

O Mary, Mother of fair love, make us love Jesus in the Blessed Sacrament as you love him!

O Mary, give us Jesus Christ now and at the hour of our death.

Aspirations encouraged by Saint Peter Julian Eymard

Prayer to Increase Eucharistic Devotion

O Virgin Mary, our Lady of the Blessed Sacrament, you who are the glory of the Christian people, joy of the universal Church, and salvation of the whole world, pray for us and awaken in all believers a lively devotion toward the most Holy Eucharist, that they may be made worthy to receive Communion daily.

With you may I adore, thank, supplicate, and console the most sacred and beloved Eucharistic Heart of Jesus!

Saint Peter Julian Eymard

Invocation for the Eucharistic Kingdom of Christ

℣. Pray for us, O Virgin Immaculate, our Lady of the most Blessed Sacrament,

℟. That the Eucharistic Kingdom of Jesus Christ may come through us!

Saint Peter Julian Eymard

O Mary, Make Me an Apostle

O Mary, Queen of Apostles, make me an apostle who bears God in my soul and radiates him to those around me. Fill my heart with such an intense love of God that I cannot keep it within myself but must communicate it to others. Make me a vessel capable of bearing Jesus Christ, that he may use me to shed light in the darkness.

O Mother, make me a temple of the Holy Trinity so that all my words, actions, prayers, gestures, and attitudes may speak of the God whom I so love. Make me an apostle, O Mary, like the great Apostle Paul. Amen.

Based on a prayer of Blessed James Alberione

Prayer of Entrustment

Mary, Queen of Apostles,
pray for us your children
who entrust ourselves entirely to you.
Pray for us so that we may never offend Jesus,
but may love him with all our hearts.
Beneath your mantle, O Mother,
we your children take refuge daily.
Make us all yours.
All that we have is yours.
You are our great teacher.
Teach us, guide us, sustain us,
defend us from every danger

as you have done until now.
And after this our exile
show us Jesus,
the blessed fruit of your womb.

Venerable Thecla Merlo, FSP

Prayer to Mary for Families

Come, Mary, and dwell in every family, which we consecrate to you.

May all families receive you with joy. May they welcome you with the same affection with which the apostle John brought you into his home after the death of your Son, Jesus.

Obtain for each family member the spiritual graces that they need, just as you brought grace to the home of Zechariah and Elizabeth.

Obtain material graces as well, just as you obtained the transformation of water into wine for the newlyweds at Cana.

Keep sin far away from every household. Be for each family light, joy, and sanctification, as you were in the family of Nazareth.

Obtain for family members an increase in faith, hope, and love, and a deeper spirit of prayer.

May Jesus, Way, Truth, and Life, dwell in every home!

Inspire everyone to follow their call and may they all be reunited in heaven one day.

Based on a prayer of Blessed James Alberione

Favorite Eucharistic Hymns

Soul of My Savior

Soul of my Savior, sanctify my breast,
Body of Christ, be thou my saving guest;
Blood of my Savior, bathe me in thy tide;
Wash me, ye waters gushing from his side.

Strength and protection may his passion be,
O blessed Jesus, hear and answer me;
Deep in thy wounds, Lord, hide and shelter me;
So shall I never, never part from thee.

Guard and defend me from the foe malign;
In death's drear moments make me only thine;
Call me and bid me come unto thy love,
Where I may praise thee with thy saints above.

O Salutaris Hostia

See page 61.

Tantum Ergo

See page 63.

O Sacrum Convivium!

O sacrum convivium,
in quo Christus sumitur:
recolitur memoria passionis eius;
mens impletur gratia,
et futurae gloriae
nobis pignus datur. Alleluia.

Ave Verum

Ave verum corpus, natum
de Maria Virgine;
vere passum, immolatum
in cruce pro homine:
cuius latus perforatum
fluxit aqua et sanguine:
esto nobis praegustatum
mortis in examine.

O Jesu dulcis!
O Jesu pie!
O Jesu, fili Mariae!

O Sacred Banquet!

O sacred Banquet,
in which Christ is received;
the memory of his passion is renewed,
the mind is filled with grace,
and a pledge of future glory is given us. Alleluia.

Saint Thomas Aquinas

Hail, True Body

Hail, true Body, born of Mary,
by a wondrous virgin-birth.
You who on the Cross were offered
to redeem us all on earth;
You whose side became a fountain
pouring forth your precious Blood,
give us now, and at our dying,
your own self to be our food.

O kindest Jesus,
O gracious Jesus,
O Jesus, blessed Mary's Son.

Attributed to Pope Innocent VI

Godhead Here in Hiding

Godhead here in hiding, whom I do adore,
Masked by these bare shadows, shape and nothing more,
See, Lord, at thy service low lies here a heart,
Lost, all lost in wonder at the God thou art.

Seeing, touching, tasting are in thee deceived:
How says trusty hearing? that shall be believed;
What God's Son has told me, take for truth I do;
Truth himself speaks truly or there's nothing true.

On the Cross thy Godhead made no sign to men,
Here thy very manhood steals from human ken:
Both are my confession, both are my belief,
And I pray the prayer of the dying thief.

I am not like Thomas, wounds I cannot see,
But can plainly call thee Lord and God as he;
Let me to a deeper faith daily nearer move,
Daily make me harder hope and dearer love.

O thou our reminder of Christ crucified,
Living Bread, the life of us for whom he died,
Lend this life to me then: feed and feast my mind,
There be thou the sweetness man was meant to find.

Bring the tender tale true of the Pelican;
Bathe me, Jesu Lord, in what thy bosom ran,

Blood whereof a single drop has power to win,
All the world forgiveness of its world of sin.

Jesu, whom I look at shrouded here below,
I beseech thee send me what I thirst for so,
Some day to gaze on thee face to face in light
And be blest for ever with thy glory's sight. Amen.

Saint Thomas Aquinas
Translated by Gerard Manley Hopkins

Panis Angelicus

Panis angelicus
Fit panis hominum;
Dat panis coelicus
Figuris terminum.
O, res mirabilis!
Manducat Dominum.
Pauper, servus et humilis.

Te trina Deitas
unaque poscimus
Sic nos tu visita
sicut te colimus
Per tuas semitas
duc nos quo tendimus
Ad lucem quam inhabitas.

Bread of Angels

Bread of Angels
Becomes the bread for all men;
The Bread of heaven
brings to an end all foreshadowings.
O, what a wonder!
The Lord becomes food
for us his poor and humble servants.

O God, One in Three
we beseech you,
come visit us, as we adore you,
guide us along your paths,
to the light wherein you dwell.

Saint Thomas Aquinas

Sing My Tongue the Savior's Glory

Sing my tongue the Savior's glory,
of his flesh the mystery sing;
of the Blood all price exceeding
shed by our immortal King,
destined for the world's redemption
from a noble womb to spring.

Of a pure and spotless virgin
born for us on earth below,
he, as man with man conversing,
stayed the seeds of truth to sow;
then he closed in solemn order
wondrously his life of woe.

On the night of that last supper,
seated with his chosen band,
he the paschal Victim eating,
first fulfills the law's command;
then as food to his apostles,
gives himself with his own hand.

Word made flesh, the bread of nature
by his word to flesh he turns;
wine into his Blood he changes—
what though sense no change discerns?
Only be the heart in earnest,
faith her lesson quickly learns.

Pange Lingua

Pange, lingua, gloriósi
Córporis mystérium,
Sanguinísque pretiósi,
Quem in mundi prétium
Fructus ventris generósi
Rex effúdit géntium.

Nobis datus, nobis natus,
Ex intácta Virgine,
Et in mundo conversátus,
Sparso vérbi sémine,
Sui moras incolátus,
Miro clausit órdine.

In suprémae nocte cenae,
Recúmbens cum frátribus,
Observáta lege plene,
Cibis in legálibus,
Cibum turbae duodénae,
Se dat suis mánibus.

Verbum caro, panem verum,
Verbo carnem éfficit:
Fitque sanguis Christi merum,
Et si sensus déficit,
Ad firmándum cor sincérum,
Sola fides súfficit.

Down in adoration falling,
Lo! the sacred Host we hail,
Lo! oe'r ancient forms departing
Newer rites of grace prevail
Faith for all defects supplying
Where the feeble senses fail.

To the everlasting Father,
And the Son who reigns on high
With the Holy Spirit proceeding
Forth from each eternally,
Be salvation, honor, blessing,
Might, and endless majesty. Amen.

Tantum ergo sacraméntum
Venerémur cérnui:
Et antíquum documéntum
Novo cedat rítui:
Praestet fides suppleméntum
Sénsuum deféctui.

Genitóri, Genitóque
Laus et jubilátio,
Salus, honor, virtus quoque
Sit et benedíctio:
Procedénti ab utróque
Compar sit laudátio. Amen.

Saint Thomas Aquinas

O Esca Viatorum

O esca viatorum
O panis angelorum
O manna coelitum.
Esurientes ciba
Dulcedine non priva
Corda quaerentium.

O lympha fons amoris
Qui puro Salvatoris
E corde profluis
Te sitientes pota
Haec sola nostra vota.
His una sufficis.

O Jesu tuum vultum
Quem colimus occultum
Sub panis specie.
Fac ut, remoto velo,
Post libera in coelo
Cernamus facie. Amen.

O Food of All Wayfaring

O food of all wayfaring,
The Bread of Angels sharing,
O Manna from on high!
We hunger; Lord, supply us,
Nor thy delights deny us,
Whose hearts to thee draw nigh.

O Stream of love past telling.
O purest fountain, welling
From out the Savior's side!
We faint with thirst; revive us,
Of thine abundance give us,
And all we need provide.

O Jesu, by thee bidden,
We here adore thee, hidden
'Neath forms of bread and wine.
Grant when the veil's divided,
We may behold, in heaven,
Thy countenance divine.

Let All Mortal Flesh Keep Silence

Let all mortal flesh keep silence,
and with fear and trembling stand;
ponder nothing earthly minded,
for with blessing in his hand,
Christ our God to earth descendeth,
our full homage to demand.

King of kings, yet born of Mary,
as of old on earth he stood,
Lord of Lords, in human vesture,
in the Body and the Blood.
He will give to all the faithful
his own self for heavenly food.

Rank on rank the host of heaven
spreads its vanguard on the way,
as the Light of lights descendeth
from the realms of endless day
that the powers of hell may vanish
as the darkness clears away.

At his feet the six-winged seraph,
cherubim with sleepless eye,
veil their faces to the presence,
as with ceaseless voice they cry,
"Alleluia, alleluia, alleluia, Lord Most High!"

Jesus, Food of Angels

>Jesus, food of angels,
>Monarch of the heart;
>Oh, that I could never
>From thy face depart!
>Yes, thou ever dwellest
>Here for love of me,
>Hidden thou remainest
>God of majesty.
>
>Soon I hope to see thee,
>And enjoy thy love,
>Face to face, sweet Jesus,
>In thy heav'n above.
>But on earth an exile,
>My delight shall be
>Ever to be near thee
>Veil'd for love of me.

Saint Alphonsus de Liguori

O God of Loveliness

>O God of loveliness,
>O Lord of heav'n above,
>How worthy to possess
>My heart's devoted love.

So sweet your countenance,
So gracious to behold,
That one, one only glance were bliss untold.

You are blest three in one,
Yet undivided still;
You are that One alone
Whose love my heart can fill.
The heav'ns and earth below
Were fashioned by Your word;
How great, how great you are, O holy Lord!

O Loveliness supreme,
And Beauty infinite!
O ever-flowing stream
And ocean of delight!
O Life by which I live,
My truest Life above,
I give you, Lord, my undivided love.

Saint Alphonsus de Liguori

Be Thou My Vision

Be thou my vision, O Lord of my heart;
Naught is all else to me save that thou art.
Thou my best thought by day and by night;
Waking or sleeping, thy presence my Light.

Be thou my wisdom, thou my true Word;
I ever with thee, thou with me, Lord.
Thou my great Father, I thy dear son;
Thou in me dwelling, I with thee one.

Be thou my battleshield, sword for the fight.
Be thou my dignity, thou my delight.
Thou my soul's shelter, thou my high tow'r;
Raise thou me heavenward, Pow'r of my pow'r.

Riches I need not, nor man's empty praise,
Thou my inheritance now and always.
Thou and thou only, first in my heart,
High King of heaven, my treasure thou art.

Heart of my own heart whatever befall,
Still be my vision, O Ruler of all.
Be thou my vision, O Lord of my heart.
Naught is all else to me save that thou art.

Attributed to Saint Dallan Forgaill

Acknowledgments

"Prayer for Priests" adapted from "Holy Thursday Letter" (1979) in *Prayers and Devotions: 365 Daily Meditations from John Paul II* by Pope John Paul II, copyright © 1984 by The K. S. Giniger Company, Inc.. Used by permission of Viking Books, an imprint of Penguin Publishing Group, a division of Penguin Random House LLC. All rights reserved.

Excerpts from the English translation of *Holy Communion and Worship of the Eucharist Outside Mass* © 1974, International Commission on English in the Liturgy Corporation. All rights reserved.

Excerpts from *The Confessions of Saint Augustine* by St. Augustine, translated by John K. Ryan, copyright © 1960 by Penguin Random House LLC. Copyright renewed © 1988 by Winona Nation and Savings Bank. Used by permission of Doubleday, an imprint of the Knopf Doubleday Publishing Group, a division of Penguin Random House LLC. All rights reserved.

A profound thanks to all the Daughters of Saint Paul who contributed in a big way to this prayer book, whether the current or earlier editions. A very special thanks to Sister Mary Leonora Wilson, who helped with the compilation and contributed some beautiful prayers, and to Sister Mary Mark Wickenhiser, who compiled and edited the 2019 edition, as well as provided many of the introductions for Part Four.

Thanks also to the many sisters who provided original prayers or source material, including:

Sister Mary Emmanuel Alves, FSP, who translated the prayer "O Immense Love" by Saint Alphonsus de Liguori

Sister D. Thomas Halpin, FSP

Sister Sharon Anne Legere, FSP

Sister Bernadette Mary Reis, FSP

Sister Virginia Richards, FSP

Sister Patricia Shaules, FSP

Sister Mary Domenica Vitello, FSP

Sister Giovannamaria Carrara, FSP

Sister Gloria Bordeghini , FSP

An extra special thanks to Sister Mary Veritas Grau, FSP, and Mary Teresa Curley for inspiring the very first editions.

Unless otherwise noted, all introductions, prayers, and reflections throughout Parts 1–3 (except the Prayers Before Mass and Prayers Before and After Communion) were authored by Sister Marie Paul Curley, FSP. Meditations on the Rosary by Sister Marie Paul Curley, FSP. Eucharistic Mysteries of the Rosary and Way of the Cross by Sister Mary Leonora Wilson, FSP.

Unless otherwise noted, all prayers in Part Four are from traditional sources.

Prayers by Blessed James Alberione are primarily from *The Prayers of the Pauline Family* (Daughters of Saint Paul, Boston.

Approved for private use. All rights reserved.) Other prayers and writings are from out of print, privately published, or non-published translations. Writings of Blessed James Alberione that are currently available in English can be found at: https://operaomnia.alberione.org/en.

Notes

1. Pope Saint Paul VI, *Mysterium Fidei*, no. 30, quoted in *Adoring Jesus with the Holy Father* (Boston: Pauline Books and Media, 2011), 20.

2. Pope Benedict XVI, *Sacramentum Caritatis* (Boston: Pauline Books and Media, 2007), no. 66.

3. *Lumen Gentium*, in Austin Flannery, O.P., ed., *Vatican Council II: The Conciliar and Post Conciliar Documents*, Study Edition (Northport, NY: Costello; Grand Rapids, MI: William B. Eerdmans, 1992), no. 11.

4. Pope Saint Paul VI, *Presbyterorum Ordinis*, The Holy See, December 7, 1965, no. 5, https://www.vatican.va/archive/hist_councils/ii_vatican_council/documents/vat-ii_decree_19651207_presbyterorum-ordinis_en.html.

5. G. K. Chesterton, "If Christ Should Come," *The Chesterton Review* 10, no. 1 (February 1984): 9, https://www.pdcnet.org/chesterton/content/chesterton_1984_0010_0001_0009_0011.

6. Blessed James Alberione, *Alle Figlie di San Paolo*, vol. 1, 1929–1933 (Rome: Figlie di San Paolo, Casa Generalizia, 2005), 541.

7. Blessed James Alberione founded the Society of Saint Paul and the Daughters of Saint Paul, who proclaim the Gospel through the media of social communication; the Sister Disciples of the Divine Master, who are dedicated to the liturgical apostolate; the Sisters of Jesus the Good Shepherd, who dedicate themselves to pastoral work;

and the Sisters of Mary, Queen of Apostles, who work to promote and guide vocations to the priestly and religious life.

8. These are the Institute of Jesus the Priest for diocesan priests, the Institute of Saint Gabriel the Archangel for laymen, the Institute of Mary Most Holy of the Annunciation for laywomen, and the Institute of the Holy Family for married couples.

9. Blessed James Alberione, *Thoughts*, trans. Aloysius Milella, S.S.P. (Boston: Daughters of St. Paul, 1974), 141.

10. Blessed James Alberione, *The Following of Christ the Master, Looking at Christ the Master, Announcing Christ the Master* (Boston: Daughters of Saint Paul), 104. Published for private use.

11. Alberione, *The Following of Christ*, 23.

12. Alberione, *The Following of Christ*, 29.

13. Alberione, *The Following of Christ*, 29.

14. Blessed James Alberione, *Until Christ Be Formed in You* (Boston: Daughters of Saint Paul), 37. Published for private use.

15. Alberione, *The Following of Christ*, 31.

16. *Sacrosanctum Concilium*, in Austin Flannery, O.P., ed., *Vatican Council II: The Conciliar and Post Conciliar Documents*, Study Edition (Northport, NY: Costello; Grand Rapids, MI: William B. Eerdmans, 1992), no. 47.

17. Pope Saint John Paul II, *Ecclesia de Eucharistia*, April 17, 2003, no. 11, https://www.vatican.va/content/john-paul-ii/en/encyclicals/documents/hf_jp-ii_enc_20030417_eccl-de-euch.html.

18. Pope Saint Paul VI, *Credo of the People of God*, The Holy See, June 30, 1968, no. 25, https://www.vatican.va/content/paul-vi/en/motu_proprio/documents/hf_p-vi_motu-proprio_19680630_credo.html.

19. John Paul II, *Ecclesia de Eucharistia*, no. 16.

20. Blessed James Alberione, *The Prayers of the Pauline Family* (Boston: Daughters of Saint Paul), 38–40. Published for private use.

21. Saint Edith Stein, "I Will Remain with You...," in *The Collected Works of Edith Stein*, vol. 4, *The Hidden Life: Hagiographic Essays, Meditations, Spiritual Texts*, ed. L. Gelber and Michael Linssen, O.C.D., trans. Waltraut Stein (Washington, D.C.: ICS Publications, 2014), 137.

22. J. R. R. Tolkien, *The Letters of J. R. R. Tolkien*, ed. Humphrey Carpenter with assistance of Christopher Tolkien (New York: Houghton Mifflin, 1981), 53.

23. Blessed James Alberione, *Daily Meditations: The Great Prayers* (Boston: Daughters of Saint Paul, 1985), 81–82.

24. Michael D. Griffin, O.C.D., comp., *Testimonies to Blessed Teresa of the Andes* (Washington, D.C.: Teresian Charism Press, 1991), 121.

25. St. Thérèse of Lisieux to Fr. Bellière (Letter 244), June 9, 1987, Archives du Carmel de Lisieux, https://www.archives-carmel-lisieux.fr/english/carmel/index.php/pere-maurice-belliere-2/11738-lt-244-a-labbe-belliere.

26. Pope Francis, "Homily of Holy Father Francis," The Holy See, May 30, 2013, no. 1, https://www.vatican.va/content/francesco/en/homilies/2013/documents/papa-francesco_20130530_omelia-corpus-domini.html.

27. Pope Francis, "Homily," no. 3.

28. Blessed James Alberione, *Practices of Piety and the Interior Life* (Boston: Daughters of Saint Paul), 245. Published for private use.

29. Daughters of Saint Paul, *May Christ Arise in Us* (2011). Private document of the Daughters of Saint Paul.

30. Pope Saint John Paul II, *Prayers and Devotions from Pope John Paul II*, ed. Bishop Peter Canisius Johannes van Lierde, O.S.A., trans. Firman O'Sullivan (New York: Viking, 1994), 236.

31. Dorothy Day, *The Long Loneliness* (New York: Harper, 1952), 285–286.

32. Ronald Rolheiser, O.M.I., "The Eucharist as Washing Each Other's Feet," Ron Rolheiser, OMI (blog), https://ronrolheiser.com/the-eucharist-as-washing-each-others-feet/#.Y-P-OnbMLct.

33. John Paul II, *Ecclesia de Eucharistia*, no. 53.

34. Prayer adapted from Constitutions and Directory of the Daughters of Saint Paul (Boston: Daughters of Saint Paul, 1984). Published for private use.

35. John Paul II, *Ecclesia de Eucharistia*, no. 58.

36. Blessed James Alberione, *Christ Lives in Me* (Boston: Pauline Books and Media, 2003), 50–51.

37. Saint Maria Faustina Kowalska, *Diary of Saint Maria Faustina Kowalska: Divine Mercy in My Soul* (Stockbridge, MA: Marian Press, 2005), no. 1692.

38. Saint Padre Pio, "Stay with Me, Lord," in *The Essential Handbook of Sacraments* (Liguori, MO: Liguori, 2001), 152.

39. John J. Cardinal Carberry, "Act of Adoration," in *Reflections and Prayers for Visits with Our Eucharistic Lord* (Boston: Pauline Books & Media, 2017), 8–9.

40. Victoria Schneider, comp. and trans., *The Bishop of the Abandoned Tabernacle: Saint Manuel Gonzalez Garcia* (New York: Scepter, 2018), 56.

41. Faustina, *Diary*, no. 1794.

42. Saint Augustine, *The Confessions of St. Augustine*, trans. John K. Ryan (New York: Image Books, 1960), bk. 10 ch. XXVII.

43. Saint Hildegard of Bingen, "Repentance and Reunion," in *Prayers of Hildegard of Bingen*, ed. Walburga Storch, O.S.B., trans. Sharon Therese Nemeth (Cincinnati, OH: Saint Anthony Messenger Press, 2003), 64–65.

44. Saint Oscar Romero, *The Violence of Love* (Farmington, PA: Plough Publishing House, 1988), 154.

45. Pope Saint John Paul II, "Letter of his Holiness John Paul II to All the Priests on the Occasion of Holy Thursday 1979," The Holy See, no. 7, https://www.vatican.va/content/john-paul-ii/en/letters/1979/documents/hf_jp-ii_let_19790409_sacerdoti-giove-di-santo.html. Adapted into prayer by Marie Paul Curley, FSP.

46. Pope Saint John Paul II, *Evangelium Vitae*, The Holy See, March 25, 1995, https://www.vatican.va/content/john-paul-ii/en/encyclicals/documents/hf_jp-ii_enc_25031995_evangelium-vitae.html.

47. Saint Peter Julian Eymard, *Month of Our Lady of the Blessed Sacrament* (New York: Sentinel Press, 1903), 21–22.

List of Contributors

SAINT MARGARET MARY ALACOQUE
  Heart of Love

BLESSED JAMES ALBERIONE
  Act of Adoration: "I adore you present in me..."
  Act of Consecration: "Receive me, O Mary..."
  Act of Faith, Hope, and Love
  Act of Faith in Jesus' Eucharistic Presence
  Act of Hope in Jesus' Eucharistic Presence
  Act of Love in Jesus' Eucharistic Presence
  Act of Resolution
  Act of Supplication
  A Eucharistic Offertory for the Media
  Chaplet to Jesus Master, Way, Truth, and Life
  God's Dream for Me
  Invocations to Jesus Master
  Invocations to the Eucharistic Heart of Jesus
  "Jesus Master, I offer my entire being to you..."
  "May you be blessed, O Jesus, who died on the cross..."
  "My Lord, I am entirely the work..."

O Mary, Make Me an Apostle
Offering of the Holy Mass
Prayer for the Gifts of the Holy Spirit
Prayer of Adoration: "Jesus, today's adoration..."
Prayer of Presence: "We adore you, Jesus, eternal Shepherd..."
Prayer to Mary for Families
To Jesus' Gentle Heart
To Jesus, Good Shepherd: "Jesus, you are the Good Shepherd..."
To Jesus, the Good Shepherd: "We thank you, Jesus Good Shepherd..."

Saint Alphonsus de Liguori
Jesus, Food of Angels
O God of Loveliness
O Immense Love!

Saint Ambrose of Milan
Prayer of Saint Ambrose Before Communion

Saint Anselm
Prayer for the Needs of Others

Saint Augustine
Possess Our Hearts
Too Late Have I Loved You

Saint Bonaventure
Prayer for Love

Sister Giovannamaria Carrara, FSP
Act of Trust in the Divine Master

Sister Gloria Bordeghini, FSP
In Our Daily Living

Cardinal John J. Carberry
Act of Adoration: "Jesus, my God, I adore you..."

Celtic Sources
You

Sister Marie Paul Curley, FSP
Act of Faith in Jesus' Promises
Act of Sorrow: "Lord, you have called me..."
Act of Sorrow: "Loving Savior, you suffered..."
An Act of Faith in the Lord's Faithful Presence
Jesus, Master, I offer my entire being to you...
Litany of Repentance
Litany of Service
Litany to Jesus Master
"Lord, I am an earthenware vessel..."
"My loving God, with all my heart I am sorry..."
The Mysteries of the Rosary: Eucharistic Reflections
Prayer of Adoration "Jesus, present everywhere..."
Prayer of Adoration, "My Jesus, Lord, I come..."
Prayer of Awareness
Prayer to Imitate Jesus, Divine Servant

"The Lord is my Master..."

CARDINAL RICHARD CUSHING
Credo, Adoro, Amo
Prayer Before the Blessed Sacrament

SAINT PETER JULIAN EYMARD
Hail Mary, of Whom Was Born our Eucharistic Jesus
Invocation for the Eucharistic Kingdom of Christ
Our Lady of the Most Blessed Sacrament
Prayer to Increase Eucharistic Devotion
Prayer to the Mother of All Adorers

SAINT DALLAN FORGAILL
Be Thou My Vision

SAINT CHARLES DE FOUCAULD
Prayer of Surrender

SAINT FRANCIS OF ASSISI
Prayer of Saint Francis
We Adore You

SAINT GERTRUDE
Prayer of Saint Gertrude for the Souls in Purgatory

ALBAN GOODIER, SJ
Praise of God's Love

MICHAEL HARTER, SJ
Novena of Grace

List of Contributors

GEORGE HERBERT
   A Grateful Heart

SAINT HILDEGARD OF BINGEN
   Repentance and Reunion

POPE INNOCENT VI
   Ave Verum / Hail True Body

SAINT JOHN CHRYSOSTOM
   I Am Not Worthy

SAINT JOHN PAUL II
   "Mary, we entrust our journey to you . . ."
   Prayer for Priests
   To Foster Respect for Life

THOMAS À KEMPIS
   Eucharistic Offering
   Prayer of Gratitude and Faith

SAINT FAUSTINA KOWALSKA
   Divine Mercy Chaplet
   Immersed in Adoration
   Prayer of Thanksgiving: "O Jesus, eternal God . . ."

MOTHER MARY LOYOLA
   Litany of Holy Communion

VENERABLE THECLA MERLO, FSP
   Act of Abandonment
   Prayer of Entrustment

SAINT LOUIS DE MONTFORT
    O Mary, My Queen

SAINT JOHN HENRY NEWMAN
    As I Walk in Your Light
    Bread of My Soul
    Shine Through Me

SAINT PATRICK
    For Protection and Enlightenment

SAINT PIO OF PIETRELCINA
    Stay with Me, Lord

HENRY AUGUSTUS RAWES, OSC
    Come, Lord Jesus

SISTER BERNADETTE M. REIS, FSP
    Forever Yours

SAINT RICHARD OF CHICHESTER
    Thanks Be to Thee

SAINT ELIZABETH ANN SETON
    Soul of Jesus

SISTER PATRICIA CORA SHAULES, FSP
    Beloved Jesus

SAINT TERESA OF AVILA
    Filled with Wonder

Saint Teresa Benedicta of the Cross
I Will Remain with You . . .

Saint Thomas Aquinas
Godhead Here in Hiding
O Sacrum Convivium
O Saving Victim / O Salutaris Hostia
Panis Angelicus
Prayer of Love and Humility
Sing My Tongue the Savior's Glory
Tantum Ergo / Humbly Let Us Voice Our Homage
Thanksgiving for the Gift of the Eucharist

Traditional
Act of Contrition: "My God, I am sorry for my sins . . ."
Act of Spiritual Communion
Angel of Fatima's Prayers of Reparation
Angelus, The
Be Merciful
Come, Holy Spirit
Divine Praises, The
Hail, Holy Queen
Jesus Prayer, The
Let All Mortal Flesh Keep Silence
Litany of Loreto
Litany of the Precious Blood
May the Heart of Jesus

Memorare

Morning Offering

O Esca Viatorum

O Sacrament Most Holy

Soul of Christ / Anima Christi

Soul of My Savior

Te Deum

To Jesus Crucified

We Fly to Your Protection

Unknown Author

Act of Desire

Act of Love and Desire

Act of Thanksgiving: "My dear Jesus, I thank you..."

Acts of Adoration, Thanksgiving, Reparation, and Prayer

Creed of the Called

For Faith in the Real Presence

Litany of Reparation to the Most Holy Sacrament

Litany of the Eucharist

Litany of the Most Blessed Sacrament

Prayer for Perseverance

Prayer of Presence "Lord, I come before you here..."

You Have First Loved Me

Sister Mary Leonora Wilson, FSP
   Act of Reparation to the Most Blessed Sacrament
   Chaplet of Eucharistic Adoration
   Eucharistic Mysteries of the Rosary
   Invocations to the Holy Spirit
   Loving Lord, I Believe
   Stations of the Cross
   To My Guardian Angel, Companion in Adoration

Pauline
BOOKS & MEDIA

A mission of the Daughters of St. Paul

As apostles of Jesus Christ,
evangelizing today's world:

We are CALLED to holiness
by God's living Word and Eucharist.

We COMMUNICATE the Gospel message
through our lives and through all
available forms of media.

We SERVE the Church
by responding to the hopes and needs
of all people with the Word of God,
in the spirit of St. Paul.

For more information visit us at:
www.pauline.org